In Defense
of Nature

sightline books...........

The Iowa Series in Literary Nonfiction
Patricia Hampl & Carl H. Klaus, series editors

In Defense of Nature

by JOHN HAY

University of Iowa Press
IOWA CITY

University of Iowa Press, Iowa City 52242
www.uiowapress.org
Copyright © 1969 by John Hay
Originally published by Little, Brown and Company, 1969
First University of Iowa Press edition, 2007

The University of Iowa Press is a member of Green Press
Initiative and is committed to preserving natural resources.
Printed on acid-free paper

Library of Congress Cataloging-in-Publication Data
Hay, John, 1915–.
In defense of nature / by John Hay.
p.   cm.—(Sightline books:
the Iowa series in literary nonfiction)
Originally published: Boston: Little, Brown. 1969.
ISBN-13: 978-1-58729-607-9 (pbk.)
ISBN-10: 1-58729-607-1 (pbk.)
1. Natural history—Outdoor books. 2. Seashore biology.
I. Title.
QH81.H37 2007   2007008842
508—dc22

To Robert Cushman Murphy

*I am most grateful to C. L. ("Joe") Barber
for his encouraging and useful criticism
during the writing of this book.*

Author's Note

I WANT to emphasize that I wrote this book not with the intention of defending "nature" as an antidote to human strain, nor did I want to linger over the natural environment only because, as a country dweller, I felt that the chipmunks and I had our backs to the wall. I live in a world that is scientifically and technologically claimed, and I am constantly obliged to employ its terms. I find that science in some instances means enlightenment and in others leads to darkness. In a technical sense, we see farther than we used to, into the flower or the star. The new sciences face us with an endless looking glass in whose corridors we see not only our own images but every detail and twitching motion of the living world, from the veined leaf to the protozoon. Of course, this ability is also a power, which can result in incalculable damage. At the same time, our seeing in might give us the opportunity to end a long night in which we as *man* have been separated from *nature* as a conquerable object.

If all our communicatory ability drives us to meet the steadfast elements of this precious and vulnerable earth at every corner, what alternative do we have but recognition? In us is the vision, the still miraculous organic experience, with which to meet the whole world of life, and not a half of it. There is a chance, in this newly defined arena of darkness and light, a chance to live and let live, a chance, paradoxically enough, to get rid of that terrible, isolating concept of man as the lord of creation. It is not so much our technical or mechanical terms that need extending but ourselves. We have a great deal of exploring to do in order to find the place where we share our lives with other lives, where we breathe and reproduce, employ our sight, and join the breadth of chances not as separate, unique entities with doomsday on our docket but as vessels for universal experience. What we call natural resources cannot be limited to gas, oil, pulpwood or uranium — we are starving the natural resources in ourselves. The soul still needs to stretch; being needs exercise.

JOHN HAY

Brewster, Massachusetts

In Defense
of Nature

I

A Dependable Endurance

Early days must have been incredibly difficult. As one resident of Rose Bay told it, "They used to get letters from home but they never answered them because their people didn't want them to go away. They thought if they'd write back and say it was so hard, why, the people'd say they had no business to come over there, and if they said it was so good, others might come. They had terrible hard times."

—Helen Creighton, *Folklore of Lunenberg County, Nova Scotia*

MORE often than not, I set out, as most of us do in the roaring twentieth century, not to walk from my house into the trees, but to open the car door. I have to begin, whether I like it or not, with what the car enables me to do. It is a symbol of society's technical domination. The highway on which it takes me out — where I have been racing half my life — leads to our means of subsistence; and it "gets you there," wherever "there" may be. Whether it has helped us communicate may be open to question. In any case, accepting it as a need, I also mean to get out of the car and stray off the highway when I can. I look for side routes that invite me to their openings, like those dusty roads whose meanderings are no longer considered vital enough to save.

I take to the road and walk down to the shore, to see those waters marked by nothing but the world winds and our onetime lord the sun. Perhaps I can claim some old attachments there. Perhaps there are old designations in me that have gone unnoticed. I make the assumption that any detail in the sky, any angle of a bird's flight, or motion in a wave, any object still not wholly felt or seen, may mean an untapped source for me, as not merely an observer but a life, in as original a sense as all other lives.

I know that man, in population, in power, now influences everything. I know that there is nothing he does not have his eyes on, nothing he does not have the capacity to move or put aside, but I also know our omnipotence has not given us much confidence in and of itself. We find we not only have the means to destroy nature but our own world too. We find that our overwhelming position does not turn us into great communicators so much as bypassers. A kind of hardening and codifying of our methods and achievements seems to have detached us from the sources of life. Direct experience of the natural earth is becoming rare. Perhaps the world of nature, because of what was once one of its own familiar predators, must now have to hold its secrets more closely than ever for survival's sake.

Still, I believe, as I set out once again, that the earth is in us, come what may, and that it has more saving examples in store than we realize, or even understand. And I suspect, as I push the car up to the speed limit, that men need something more than speed to get them where they need to go.

I drive through the city, the great smoking heap of civilization, with gas in my nostrils, a roaring beside me and overhead, the human imagination and order embodied all around me as cars, planes, factories, concrete hives, miles of glass, countless lights, a huge fantasy-filled horizon spewing out poverty and grime on its fringes, belching tons of waste into the atmosphere. This order may contain power on its own, charged by what it takes and consumes, a vast greed, hardly aware of where the original fuel may have come from that fires its furnaces. But I know that wherever man took his violent path in the first place he is inextricably a part of universal energy, and there is no way out.

We have not conquered nature, any more than I have conquered myself. Life unfinished is the rule for man or trees. What I go looking for is not nature under man's control but a wider, lasting range — that which we will have to live with in order to avoid a life in isolation, that which belongs to us only when we go out to meet it.

Americans have certainly gone far since yesterday, when this continent meant an almost impenetrable shoreline confronting a few men in a wooden ship. It does seem strange that just behind all the headlong and scarcely understood exploitation of energy, the rush not to be late, the readiness to be run over, this was a rough, raw, untamed land to which the earliest voyagers came like wolves pawing gingerly around a cache of frozen meat.

Suddenly, in the age of crescendo, we seem to have jettisoned several centuries of New World history which for terror, conflict, and cliffs of human experience have never had adequate embodiment in our literature. Perhaps sometimes, when the wind is blowing from the right quarter and the surf roars, you can imagine cries of rage, distress, greed, and protests to the Almighty, but the echoes seem to be growing fainter every day. It is true that the woodlands are coming back in many areas, and that there is still a residue of farmland, of barns and the stone wall culture, gaunt and at the same time redolent of all seasons, comforting; but the pastoral strength of our recent past does not mean a great deal to us. We have an inheritance in America of leaving continuity behind before it has a further chance to develop, and in part this has been because a vast new continent gave us space to fill, and kept us going before we even knew we had to stop. It was in part a conquest by right of the conquered. In that sense, we had a close, warring relationship with the land, before a later day when it was not so much fought as covered over and ignored.

The past meant war, an all-out attack on the dark riches of a new land. In Maine and Canada, still relatively untouched by urban sprawl, evidences of their Antietams, their Verduns and their Okinawas are plain to see. The battlefields show us great areas of bare rock-bones, partly covered by alder, gray birch and goldenrod. In other regions just the powerful beauty of woods and shore is eloquent enough about what the would-be conquerors faced when they arrived.

On some of the less protected shores facing the North Atlantic great round boulders jostle each other in the surf. Stormy seas pound on upthrust blocks of rock and toss spray over the shoulders of granite sloping down to the water. High curtains of rain or impenetrable snow move across the hills above cliffs and stony coves, and the wind shears through the tunnels of the spruce. Three hundred and more years ago the dangers of the sea were commonplace for most Europeans. It was a familiar realm, in legend or reality. But what lay behind this somber, shrouded coastline, those precipitous, gray and dark green heights with plunging wave lines below them? Some men landed and made their independent way. And some were landed, like those seventeenth-century German settlers who were promised milk and honey before they left their homeland, then fleeced of their money and crowded into ships where there was often so little room and food as to result in famine, cannibalism and suicide. Aside from the actual hardship of immediately scraping into the rocky topsoil of Maine for a living, what did they feel with the weight of a colossal, still unconquered land at their backs? The unbroken forests were full of unknown dangers, and to many they presented a witch-haunted, horrifying darkness. In some parts of America the settlers laid the land completely bare to the pitiless sun simply because they hated and despised the trees, even blaming their shade for sickness and death. The trees were felled from the Atlantic to the Pacific, thousands and thousands of square miles of them, not only for the need of cleared land, building and firewood, but also because they stood in the way and had to be fought to the limit.

The American landscape rolled on ahead — forests, rivers, plains and lakes, mountains and deserts — open, grand, invigorating, sometimes menacing, stormy and wide, rich in hazards, rich in detail, and every new battle or meeting with it meant that the experience of the natural wilderness had added to our stature. When the war was won, the experience was ended, but we are still trading on its impetus. We "conquerors" will get what stature we can, though it may be spurious, from universal possession.

The land has new proprietors; and will they ever know it well enough? Will they be able to value the earth not only for its products, its man-made triumphs, but for what it is? We are not so nearly on speaking terms with nature as we used to be. Common naming, common names, are less familiar. Timber-doodles, shitepokes, ragged robins, skunk coots, walleyed herring and quawks are disappearing into books. How can the three-quarters of our population that lives in cities replace such terms, and all the humorous, rough, gentle, accurate acquaintance they imply? Common naming means a common recognition that numbering will never find. The object needs a person, to be personified.

The natural environment lacks the security of our once familiar speech, and we have also become less amazed, perhaps in the process of this loss. The earth no longer comes before us in a new aspect with every hidden flower and every earth-regenerating clap of thunder. We have left a great deal of awe behind us. The fact that we can alter and remake the environment almost at will has deprived us of much of our original surprise in its manifestations, even though it kicks back at us from time to time. To be a "free agent," in idea if not in fact, is to be tempted into monumental carelessness.

It is becoming rare to find communities still founded on a common experience that grew out of the land they settled in. To the north, in regions which are gradually less populated as you progress, the old ways may be easier to recapture, even to the superstitions. The harsh, dangerous, seagoing life of the New England seaboard and the Canadian Maritimes once encouraged a wealth of belief in mirages, presences and strange disappearances. Like the Indians, the local people used to believe in charms and countercharms, and they swore by stories about "forerunners," supernatural happenings that told of a coming disaster. Underneath common reality, in the air, superstitious feelings were handed down through local generations of people, almost electrically communicated.

It may be hard for a contemporary man, rid of most superstitions (if not tribal routines), to believe that places existed not long ago where ghosts were real. But when I heard a Canadian say, "Every time I see a dead person I have to wash my hands before I can eat again," I felt that I was back in the subsistence struggle and the world of the spirits.

Superficially, the north country looks as though it were just as much affected by human presence as any other place, but it still imposes a climatic rigor, a semi-isolation, with a will of its own. During my sporadic trips there I have often had a sense of primal age, held in its own right by bold, raw rock, cold, swinging seas, a silvery sky, whose force now and force behind seem to be as ready to have men relate themselves to the sky by myth and magic as any scientific progress by plotting arcs into the unknown. Nature to the south is often disguised as "vacation land." In the north it requires some attention to its own authority.

One afternoon, in the northern part of Cape Breton, I walked off a side road to look for a beaver dam up a small stream that ran through a meadow and marsh backed up by a bowl of hills. It was in early spring. The snow which lay over the forested banks on either side of the little valley was still deep. The season's air was cool and circumspect, but there were signs of a gradual release. Patches of snow were melting away in the sun in the more level and open areas along the stream, revealing last year's leaves and patches of moisture-soaking moss. Fleas, gun-metal gray, flocked over sun-warmed snow. Where the stream's rounded white covers of snow and ice were melted, the golden-brown waters rushed down, and in side pools there were water striders flicking and twitching over the surface, making little leaf-like dimples. I heard a hemlock bough jerk lightly behind me, and turned, thinking of a bird, to see only that the bough had been released from a burden. The spruce and hemlock, with their rough bark, and their needle-lattices that shaded and saved the snow on the ground, were letting it slip slowly from their branches. Below them were clumps of alder with hanging gold-tinted catkins.

The stream's cold waters poured on. In open areas the trees spired against a radiantly blue sky, and light breezes blew over the ground. A wild woodland robin screamed and fled away ahead of me. Then I saw the big paw marks of a lynx in the snow and I began to track it up the bordering banks until the drifts were too deep. On my way back I was followed by a golden-crowned kinglet which seemed to have no fear of me at all. It kept flitting over my head, flying quickly around the clearings between the trees and coming back again, expressing itself in high, thin notes all the time, a tiny olive-green bird, with light gray under-parts and a stripe on its head like a flick of fire.

A little later I found a few beaver-chewed logs lying loosely over the stream, with clumps of brush fixed to them, but not the animal itself. Everything I saw, or that met me, seen or unseen, in that short walk, brought a recognition out of me, clear and positive in depth. I saw intricate alliances of crystal light in the needles of the evergreens, over snow running through sun and shade, across flowing banks and ravines, cold pools under the ice, warm ones in the sunlight, over craggy shadows, open yellow grasses, past waters mellifluous and laced with light. I thought of all the visitors here, the lynx with its silver eyes, the deer that stepped in on slender legs to drink, a snowshoe hare, or a tramping man, throughout the extremes of the seasons: a fury of flies, water roiled in flood, the massive snow. Kinglet or water strider, lynx track and catkin, the stream and its traces, the rooted trees, the little fish or migrant birds, came to this place or lived here; and all made it live, each to its chance, in the balance of chances. In this small valley was a power and surety that met all random events, all accidents, as they came on, and it was no tyranny . . . fragility, sensitivity, connectedness, were a part of it. This also meant inches, feet, acres joining thousands of miles of procedural events, an orderly provision in which every action was accepted into space. With the black, inquisitive little eyes of the kinglet glancing at me quickly, I had thought to myself that in the perfection of this place you might as well live eight minutes or eighty years. When the stars appeared at night over the hills and the spruce, everything I had seen, from point to point, in significant detail, seemed to join those flaming stations of light, as inadvertently as breath.

It may be true that we can only be taken up into the precision and wholeness of nature on occasion, often by accident, and sometimes as a result of practice, preparing ourselves for whatever openings may come. If we are only fractionally committed in the first place, that may be the best we can expect. Men go their own way, and nature's "blind" entities do not always seem to be relevant to human endeavor. We drive through valleys and rip through woods on journeys to which we can always attribute a human end, seldom stopping to ask our way of things that can obviously give no answers, except by our leave. We have our terms, as nothing else does, our own conscious ability to explain success or failure, our supra-natural methods to help us command our surroundings. We pass by a nature that continues with this seemingly cool, ageless use of elements, the kinglet, the water and the moss, and to personalize them, in an age of man-centered progress or apocalypse, may seem irrelevant, even trivial.

In other words, for reasons of indifference, for reasons of self-preoccupation, for reasons of haste, men act as if they only met nature when they were ready to. But when I watched the kinglet, or the wind shake the evergreens, what did I have to start with except what was theirs to give *me*? How, also, could I know them unless we were together in a realm of knowing, unless our world was mutual? Our perception of things depends on what they are, in their essence, not on man's disposal of them. Alliances, between men, between men and nature, do not last in one-sided terms. In order to know any other part of being, I am obligated to give way. When night falls, how can I truly answer its silence but by silence? When the stars began to shine and frost settled down over the ground in Nova Scotia, and a world in unity seemed to appear before me, what did I have at my back but a dependable endurance that supported everything without exception, and no one for his arguments, or his special virtues?

2

For the squid, whose nature is to come by night, as well as by day, I tell them I set him a candle to see his way, with which he is much delighted, or else cometh to wonder at it, as do our fresh-water fish. The other cometh also in the night but chiefly in the day, being forced by the cod that would devour him, and therefore, for fearing of coming so near the shore, is driven dry by the surge of the sea on the pebble and sands. Of these, being as good as a smelt, you may take up with a shove-net, as plentifully as you do wheat in a shovel, sufficient in three or four hours for a whole city.

> "A Letter written to Mr. Richard Hakluyt of the Middle Temple, Containing a Report of the True State and Commodities of Newfoundland." *Hakluyt's Voyages*, 1578

I HAVE to travel at intervals just to prove to myself that the valley was its intricate alliances or an Atlantic cove rimmed by the glory of high weather is still there, though I do not always go on my own terms. It might be better to give up the car and walk permanently, but I have my attachments. The ganglia of communications have me by the neck. Never out of reach of a newspaper, TV set, plane, electric light, telephone, or perhaps an unseen tapping device, I have a modern helplessness which often stops me before I start.

Contemporary travel has a curiously anesthetizing, self-enclosed quality. You can go several hundred miles in the wrong direction, as I once did to my embarrassment, and if you get the next flight back, not lose more than a couple of hours. The fantastic but hardly noticed speed, the dark-suited passengers reading the stock market quotations as if they were not flying over the edge of a great sea or complex landscape at all but were in a city bus — even the possibility of an unregarded death, makes travel not so much a matter of bypassing time and distance as losing track of transitions. We take our cities with us and join them together as we go. It amounts to a new kind of insularity. Speed past sound, forced immediacy, puts all the world in the same room.

Have we become so megalopolitan as to lose our innate responses to whatever distinctive part of the earth we call home? Fiddler crabs have been transported from one coast to another, with entirely different tides, or put in receptacles of still, nontidal water, and their behavior has continued to be timed exactly to the tidal rhythms of their home flats. Then, gradually, though they were as insulated from the outside as a scientist knew how to make them, they sensed the atmospheric changes around them and adjusted their reactions to the lunar periods with which such changes are rhythmically allied. Insulation, self-installed, seems to work better with us in keeping us detached from the inner rhythms and senses of this planet. We seem to have lost the kind of inner timing which makes the plant react to the changes in the season, which sends the migrant herring or salmon to find its home stream, or the tern to leave a northern coast and fly down the shores of an entire continent. We still have the tides in us of our natal blood, but I sometimes wonder whether our conscious correspondence with them has not been left behind.

After one such trip I got into my car and drove home. There was a smoky sunset on the hills, wind stirred the pines beyond the city. I saw a rare man out walking by himself in a field, and I felt that this natural, landed part of things, with all its relative speeds, from a turtle to a hawk, was not only like an old culture left behind, but that it had become fictionalized.

On the other hand neither jet nor rocket can reduce the earth's surpassing age. Perhaps they even emphasize it. One spring I flew in to Newfoundland, over the water from Cape Breton, past miles of drift ice that hugged the coast. On the approaches to the great island itself, the sunset made a blazing coppery path across ice and sea, a series of amazing spots and shines. The mountains inland from the coast were like flat-topped piles of brown earth, veined with stony streams, sometimes radiating down to ponds and lakes. It was a landscape interminably grooved and grained, and bore no resemblance to the aerial views between Boston and Washington, where you look down on a man-scarred earth, the thin, worn lip of land along the sea covered with grids made by houses and roads, smoking with the human atmosphere. I had never seen such irregularity. It was earth stress and change in relief, an old world bitter and mighty, and, as night came on, cavernously dark.

After a short spring visit, I came back in July. One late afternoon at Cape Spear, which faces the open Atlantic south of St. John's, the headlands were almost completely closed in by fog, though I could see a few kittiwakes flying close by inshore, and swinging down to fish. (The kittiwake breeds on clamorous, fog-shrouded islands off the coast, along with other sea-birds, but it is a true ocean wandering gull which spends the rest of the year far at sea. Newfound-landers call it "tickle-lace" and "lady-bird." These small gulls are pearly gray and white with sharp black on their wing tips and banded tail feathers, and when they fly over the water fishing, wing-rowing neatly and quickly, dipping and turning, they belong to the word *grace* like no other birds I ever saw.) Once a minute my ears were split by the bawling, bass note of a foghorn close by. On the short-summered land various kinds of heath were only just in bloom. There were tiny pink flowers on mountain cranberry and lowbush blueberry, white flowers on the Labrador tea. I heard the alarm note of a trim, tail-wagging water pipit as I climbed a boulder-strewn hillside full of buttercup and clover. In and out of the rocks and the wisps of blowing fog, underneath and beyond me, I felt the ancient landscape, the flow and tilt and weight of millions of years.

This coastal ground and the ground beyond it had been scoured by glaciers like no other I had seen. Some of the mountains were already eroded to the butt before the glaciers came and now looked like piles of rubble, thinly covered by vegetation. The sea's edge at the outlet of rivers and streams, or former streams, was full of the wash of loose earth and stone. Shattered slate and sandstone fell down the eroded slopes. I had been shown one high wall above a cove, whose sheer face had marks of ripples made by the sea 600 million years before. In other areas volcanic rock and sandstone were oddly juxtaposed. Without having any precise knowledge of geology, I could see enough to be deeply struck by the unimaginable stress and at the same time tidal order of earth processes — growth, fire and ruin in a mountainside, on the classic scale. We move together on a violent shore.

There was a silvery light over the great rounded boulders where the surf washed back and forth with a kind of lazy largesse. Kittiwakes showed occasionally through the fog. Then the wind changed and it began to clear toward six o'clock. A short rainbow, shaped like a horseshoe, appeared over the water. I had heard this called a "fog eater" by a Nova Scotian coming over on the ferry from Maine. "You see one of these," he said, "you feel good. It's going to clear." And as the "fog buster" (another version from Newfoundland) shone out and the curtains of fog began to lift, I could see the steady drifting by in wide and easy circles of the gulls, diving as they went, and beyond them many more making white rafts on the water's surface.

Then, in a direction where there had been nothing to be seen all afternoon, the outlines of a big, deep Newfoundland dory appeared, and in it were three fishermen casting handlines over the side. I could not help thinking of the long history behind them, of the thousand years and more, starting presumably with the Norse, that European fishermen and explorers had touched on this coast and grappled with it, with a rough acceptance of extreme endurance, through ice, fog, shipwreck, famine and drowning, of which most of us can have little conception. Hakluyt's *Voyages* speaks of the Newfoundland "Cod, which alone draweth many nations thither, and is become the most famous fishing of the world." And there is mention of the Banks off the coast where: "The Portugals, and

French chiefly, have a notable trade of fishing . . .
where are sometimes an hundred or more sailes of
ships: who commonly beginne the fishing in Apriell,
and have ended by July. That fish is large, alwayes
wet, having no land neere to drie, and is called Corre
fish.

"During the time of fishing, a man shall know without sounding when he is on the banke, by the incredible multitude of sea foule hovering over the
same, to prey upon the offalles & garbish of fish
thrown out by the fishermen, and floting upon the
sea."

(Not long ago in Normandy the discontinuance of
the Pardon of the Newfoundlanders was reported in
the news, and another direct link, in custom and re-
ligion, between man and his earthly food seems to
have been lost. This rite, also called the Pardon des
Terres-Nuevas, used to be performed for Basques,
Bretons or Normans from as early as the sixteenth
century, and probably before that. It is recorded that
the Spanish were employing experienced Breton
pilots to take them to the Grand Banks in 1511. Each
year the fishing boats were blessed and the towns-
people made a procession to the shore before seeing
their men off across the lonely, gray steppes of the
Atlantic.)

And now, as if to show its own lasting continuity,
the big body of a cod plunged straight up and dropped
back heavily into the water, where the wind made

silvery and dark patches, rainlike on the clearing surfaces of the sea. Beyond it I saw that the fishermen were pulling in dark bodies of codfish hand over hand almost continuously, throwing out their lines and quickly hauling them in again. In the middle of this display of inshore bounty, of the advantage taken of the sea's intermittent giving, a big old man in the boat saw me watching from the hillside and waved over, with a great smile on his face. A new moon appeared in the sky and a fiery red sun started to disappear behind the coastal shoulders jutting out into the sea.

There was a calm wordlessness over the water, a savage evening brightness, the presence of quick life, quick death, multitudes of fish, birds, and fishing men brought there by inexorable greed, balanced by the ages; and it was not something we ask for necessarily, as part of the acceptable world, but I took it as an offering, in answer to all need. In this exposed country, at the sea's eye, in the sea's hand, the underlying wildness, the undefiled depth could show itself. I felt that I had been profoundly welcomed there. I was at home.

II

The Pace of the Tides

WE are inclined to see the contemplation of nature in its balanced amplitude as a luxury that we have to go far to enjoy. Our back doors are walls that hide the sky. We are almost entirely surrounded by objects, goods and images of our own making, and what attachment can this newly artifacted world have with the one outside it, composed of mere trees, scared rabbits and inanimate rock?

It is certain that the closeness of men and the natural earth as we once knew it, in the sense of local need and local routine, is largely going. There are still fishermen who are with their fish, in cold, raw weather, and people to whom their daily bread is a blessing because they have baked it themselves, but they have become scarce. Sowing the seed, watching its growth, struggling, in and around the year, with the exactions of the year, has relatively few practitioners. There may be no use going into mourning for hardscrabble farm, but the anonymous company which replaced it has no better hands with which to take up a hoe, or eyes for the wind. The farmers and the fishermen were often highly skilled professionals. They learned a reality, and they learned it in terms of living with place . . . something that is not taught by substitutes, on short acquaintance.

One of my regular stops along the coast, where my family takes its vacations, is on the shores of a cove in Maine. Almost every day when we are there I can see one old man walk down to the town landing to dig clams. He has been doing it all his life. Slowly, with shoulders bent, he walks down the road from his house. When he gets to the landing he picks up two hods, wooden, slatted, clam baskets, and then moves down to the rim of wet, gray tidal flats, made of muddy clay and stones and a residue of shells and detritus and starts to dig. Or else he gets into his old skiff, starts the outboard, and heads off to a farther stretch of shore around the borders of the wide cove, an inland entrance to tidal waters rising in and ebbing back through inlets and islands out of the open sea.

Aside from a few lobster pots which he tends, and a few dollars which he may pick up for pulp wood from his own already skinned land, clamming is his almost constant occupation, even during the winter months. This same area once had a soft-shell clam industry which occupied many men and was valued at $150,-000 a year. Now there are only a relatively few men who moor their boats just offshore and make as much of the tidal grounds beyond them as they can, fitting their efforts to the vagaries of the market price from year to year and the fluctuating supply. For the amount they receive they need very strong backs, or some extra means of earning a living. Digging clams is part of a persistence as much as subsistence, economy.

It can be said that this is a sick industry compared with what it used to be, and a risky one to depend on. Just a few miles down the shore, where towns or boating areas are located, shellfish may be put off limits at any time, banned because of pollution. Because of many years of over-digging and bad digging practices, the clams are in fairly short supply to begin with, though they have a remarkable power to recuperate. But lamentations are not altogether in order for a trade through which men can still have a hand in what they gather. The clammers may not be as deprived as some of the rest of us who are ignorant of the kind of communality that goes with food gathering. When the men, young and old, come in with their dories to meet the wholesaler's truck, any onlooker will soon see and hear that there is amity and rich experience in the collection and distribution of the soft-shell clam. There is a touch of freedom to clamming, a leftover from an earlier day whose local worlds were large and self-sufficient, not dependent on a vast, impersonal market, less affected by needs not visibly connected with their own. For all that can be said about the narrowness and meanness of rural life, men talked together.

That freedom was not only what the Glorious Fourth meant to a small town but it was also that of a casual fisherman, who had no special hours but worked when he wanted to, and when weather, tides and food supply permitted him. He was a man who would have a hard time adjusting to regular hours and a steady job. He had a special working arrangement with the world of nature. He cherished some secrets with relation to it, and had a corresponding inner weather. Such a man has been deserted by the world. Some of his descendents, inheriting the casual, may have lost the freedom, and their idleness lacks support. It is like those teen-age country boys who spend half their time racing up and down the road in old cars, which they fix up with spare parts and then discard, leaving their wreckage strewn in the fields. An angry deprivation shows in them, often directed at a world that races off in the distance on its own indefinite ways, beyond their means to connect with it. They act obliquely toward it by taking out the wreck, gunning the motor, roaring down the road and back again.

Meanwhile, the old clammer, still threaded to a poor but perhaps more stable past whose values seemed to grow by slow accretion, walks slowly down the shore. In a world of space-time, his is a one-place, life-span continuum. While satellites take pictures of the earth from twenty-five thousand miles up as it revolves through space, covered by swirling clouds, the old man sits down on a rock to rest. While laboratory minds, aided by computers, project their causal methodology into the future, he may be dreaming of the past. While science moves toward harnessing the methods of the sun through nuclear fusion and attaining unlimited energy for mankind, he stands, legs apart, head and shoulders down, intently and thoroughly digging away with his clam fork, working over the ground section by section.

He has a lined and craggy face, with a stub of a nose extending from it, and a wide mouth that can extend into a Socratic grin. Thin hanks of gray hair hang over the back of his neck from under his cap. While he makes brief comments about local trouble or short-time observations about the weather, his voice gargles from a depth. Tired, with a certain sad humor in him, he seems to last, without comment, the way the tides do; but he is also part of the talk around him, generations of it defined by that swinging back and forth, the ebb and flow:

"Where'd you find that quahog?"

"Wasn't it awful about that boy that drownded!"

"Two of 'em, wan't it? Cousins."

"Don't pay to be too careless."

"Back here tomorrow, now, when the tide's up."

I suppose, in terms of a society that prides itself on replacement, that the old man is a leftover from a nonreturnable age. On the other hand, judgments of that kind are subject to their own limitations. There are constants, growth, aging and death, that have to be known in any era of man's history — they are a part of history — and if technological urgency separates us from them it does not mean that we may not have to return some day. There is a fitness in natural experience, an intimacy, that may not be superseded. How many, in this world of devices, now live through a lifetime of tides, nights of clean wind and clear stars above the roofline, know genuine exposure to cold rain, cold water and stiff fingers, know how to be steady there? Are you not also made of what you receive?

A great blue heron, which the old man calls a "crane," as the early settlers did, flies in over an inlet off the cove. Its great wings flap slowly between glides. Its long body is dark and smoky across the gray December sky, with its breast bunched and hanging like a pouch, legs and curled feet stretching straight out behind. As it goes by it causes a flurry in a flock of little black and white buffleheads which are ducking and swimming around in the water. They all veer off at once, spreading hurriedly over the surface like a fan. Some of the dark, conical rocks along the shore are plated with ice that cracked on top when tidewaters lifted and lowered, giving them the appearance of giant barnacles. Above the rocks the ranked spruce stand thick and hardy with whips of white birch showing between them.

His flat-bottomed skiff was partially frozen in during the night, so the old man wades down into the thick skin of slushy ice that sheathes the rim of the cove, with high waders on, pulling the boat's painter so that the soft ice spurts up as the rope is ripped free. Then he rocks the skiff loose and pulls it steadily and slowly out to open water, having first thrown in three clam baskets, and then rows out to the far side of the cove, backwatering with his oars. Even at fifteen above zero, these things are attended to, evenly and methodically. When the skiff is grounded on an underlying rock, he rocks the boat calmly while turning it around with one oar to release it, as if this were a matter of old routine.

The tide ebbs. Sunlight begins to bloom through ranks of heavy, early morning clouds, lighting up a big flock of herring gulls that circle round and round above the water, whose silvery surfaces are marked by the occasional dark accents of ducks flying fast and low. The clam flats glisten. They are covered with patches of snow and ice, clumps of rockweed, stones, beds of blue mussels, rock ledges that will be covered with seals next summer, and beyond are corners after islanded corners, with spruce ranked on rims of granite, out to the open sea.

There is in these regions a turning and hesitating, a waiting evidenced in birds or men, slack tide and full tide, the sunlight showing and then fading again, color and light on the sea, changing, moving on the order of the weather. The tide, which shows here as a final impulse, the end manifestation of a great tidal wave in the open ocean, a blister on the earth's surface pulled by the moon, is tangible. It tells men when to go out and when to come in, although the men I have watched along the shore, pulling their boats out at just the right time before ice moves in with the tide, or before a flood tide, and as they set out and come back with rhythmic assurance, do not need to be told.

At intervals the tide shows something of its great power as well as its well-timed motion. Giant volumes of water have to be forced through inlets and channels during every incoming tide. In late winter, commonly in March, when local tides are exceptionally high, they lift tons of ice off the rock ledges along the shore, and tidal currents, moving at six or seven knots, can take this ice so that it shoves against wooden pilings and may have the effect of sawing them off. Through various channels, wide and narrow, at all times of the year, tidewater swirls around rocks and headlands, and the surface tosses with conflicting currents that also sweep past the shore, rushing hard, sometimes making whirlpools as they go.

All the way from the open sea with its winds, its larger waves and rolling distances, to a sheltered inland cove, there are many gradations and levels of shifting waters. To the eye at least, these stretches make anything but a continuous level. They seem to plane off from horizon to horizon. And of course they may be turbulent in one channel and calm in an adjoining one. You round one island in a boat, coming closer to the sea, and the wind stiffens, the water shivers and roughs up; or in summer after the land heats up during the day there is an onshore breeze in the afternoon to cause waves on calm and sheltered waters. At any time of the year there are different belts of temperature and turbulence across these bays, inlets and islands invaded by the sea.

The tides rotate around the day, the year, the centuries, keeping their mathematical, graceful pace, to be reckoned accurately for whatever part of the coast we live in. I have heard it said that the tides, more than anything else, made men feel the imprisoning of the universe, meshed in its gears and no escape. But the wheels within this wheel are infinitely variable, infinitely discoverable. The overall weather roams and turns. Birds hesitate, fly out, wheel overhead, land and feed. The flock of buffleheads, white feathers glistening in gray light, suddenly whip up off the running shallow waters of the cove. Everything changes, gives, adapts at any given moment. When change is watched for, when it is seen as an associative process, and not a goal, then it can show us more room, instead of less.

If I leave the clam diggers behind I go back to a world which we seem to manipulate for manipulation's sake. Relative to our overcoming of distance, the sun rises in the west and sets in the east. We chase the dust of the universe. We are capable not only of losing time but freezing it. In our intellectual vanity, mortality is an illusion and age is not significant. Sometimes I think of the old man back there, bent over and legs apart, as a kind of Hercules still carrying *his* known world on his shoulders.

At the same time this disenchantment with a steady earth carries certain lasting realities with it. No amount of material conquest, nothing that our "noosphere" can do, seems to help the poor human animal as he not only flees from violence, but runs blindly and unerringly into its arms. Nothing seems to prevent human power from having to obey its own terrible logic, nothing seems to call cruelty to task but its own outcome. Crisis and disaster may be our only educators. We seemed to have learned nothing. Our domination over nature is a self-invented myth, and all we have succeeded in doing is to make ourselves outsiders, or perhaps it is more accurate to say one-siders, with respect to the teeming, multi-millennial life of earth; but is it not from this common life, these mysteries of human action that we start? Perhaps to know and acknowledge deprivation and mortal illusion is a way to order, where the natural level is the level of human need. The pace of the tides is a constant, to be learned again.

III

"Teach Us to Care"

The basic question is whether a hawkless, owl-less country-side is a livable countryside for Americans with eyes to see and ears to hear. . . . Is a wolfless north woods any north woods at all?
— Aldo Leopold, *Sand County Almanac*

WE have developed a phenomenal ability to play hide and seek with the rest of nature, or to avoid it completely. We do not think we have to meet it face to face, unless disaster comes along, and then we can blame it for not staying in its cave where we left it; and this is the cave of rational dissection as well as exploitation. But as doom will out when least expected, in the form of an earthquake, an avalanche, or a flood, so the incomparable character of a life not made by man may suddenly hit us between the eyes, the free rarity of creation, the thing which through our ignorance we may cause to disappear. When we stop caring about the irreplaceable we will have lost more than the great auk or the Carolina parakeet.

Much has been said or written about the extinct passenger pigeon, and after all, clouds of them darkened the sky within living memory, and broke off branches of trees with their weight. Forbush wrote that "it was in some respects the finest pigeon the world has seen," and it was commensurate in its incredible numbers with the spread of forests across a matchless continent.

"They migrated *en masse*. That is, the birds of one great nesting rose into the air as one body, and the movements of these immense hosts formed the most wonderful and impressive spectacle in animated nature. There were stirring sights in this and other countries when great herds of grazing animals thundered over the plains, but the approach of the mighty armies of the air was appalling. Then vast multitudes, rising strata upon strata, covered the darkened sky and hid the sun, while the roar of their myriad wings might be likened to that of a hurricane; and thus they passed for hours and days together, while the people in the country over which the legions winged their way kept up a fusillade from every point of vantage. Where the lower flocks passed over high hilltops, people were stationed with oars, poles, shingles, and other weapons to knock down swarming birds, and the whole countryside was fed on pigeons until the people were surfeited."

There are few multitudes left, other than in the human species or the insects, which keep escaping our attempts to kill them off, to deserve the term "appalling." The tragedy is that many of the standards by which the majesty of the earth could be judged have been cut down. Attention has to be given not to natural life in the fullness of things but to conserving a remnant, and the human record for restraint is nothing to count on. In fact, we are none too good at noticing what we have left. Some national attention may be directed toward saving the whooping crane, but it seems hard for us to count the robins in our own backyards.

Conservation, along with world poverty, ought to get all the support that is reserved for war and supersonic jets; but there are times when I wonder what the term means, or if its meaning has not been so dimmed by public usage that it has lost some of its efficacy in the process. Because conservation is in the public domain, it runs the political risk of having too many faces and facing in too many different directions. The basic question is what we think it important to conserve, and if we can only answer that in terms of our own economic and technological demands we may find that we have left out most of earth and our own sustenance. How can we put our overwhelming utilitarian world, with all its automatic functions, in the right relation with an earth whose provenance and integrity it disregards? If it is our intention to save open space, will it be saved for its own sake or for "public use," and how do you define what the public needs in any other terms than those of public pressure?

It is very difficult, and often justifiably so, to make people believe in a balanced alliance between them and the natural world when they feel that their own wants and livelihood might be impaired by it. We have not been effectively persuaded that our livelihood, even our sanity, depends on a natural environment which is allowed its own proper growth and functions. We have not been taught that our replacements of ecological systems have on the whole left the world much poorer than it used to be. We have not been educated in the fact that our livelihood depends not only on the conservation of open areas but on recognition of the diverse standards of natural existence everywhere, without exception.

Conservation should be against the impoverished and denuded world which man is threatening. Its name should stand out clearly in favor of an earthly society where men and nature do not simply coexist in uneasy terms but live together. Any politically involved movement is bound to compromise, but there is a point beyond which conservation cannot compromise and fulfill itself. It cannot backtrack from a fundamental stand against the careless and arbitrary dismissal of living species on this planet. The least we can do, whatever we think of ourselves as capable custodians of the earth environment, is to put our emphasis on caring whether these lives continue or not.

They come down to us unequaled. Since we have a major effect on their habitat we have a major responsibility toward them, and in the long run their survival has a direct connection with our own. This inherited earth habitat, after all, is mutually involved, mutually dependent, but proud in its complexity. It is not just divisible into man and his economic slaves.

To conserve and have it stick needs more education in particularity and in close attention to the precious elements of life than we have yet had. An effective association is what is lacking, to back such education up. Who knows how great a depth is taken away from us when we cut down a century-old grove of trees, or how much opportunity, how much exceptional insight, will depart with a bluebird or a duck hawk? A weak argument perhaps, to those who think creation begins and ends with human beings, but they should know what nature knows, that no one species can count on survival in isolation from all others, even its predators.

Do we know what we are losing? Hardly a day passes when our futurists are not congratulating us on living to be a hundred and twenty, or piping salt or mountain air into the living room — so that we never need leave it, presumably — while our resources, the earth's and ours, slip away almost invisibly. Not long ago someone shot another osprey. This was during the fall season for game birds, which seems to be getting more and more indiscriminate as to targets while the guns and the ammunition supply increase. In any case, the osprey, whether it was shot willfully or by mistake, was damaged in one wing and brought in to our local natural history museum to be cared for. There I saw it in its cage, and thought of the problems of its race.

The osprey or fish hawk was once enormously abundant in this country. In fact it has a worldwide range, depending on a continuous supply of fish wherever they can be found, both in fresh water lakes and rivers and the shallow waters of the seacoast. It should be noted that the problem of its conservation is by no means new. In some parts of the world hunters and egg collectors nearly exterminated it a long time ago. It is still almost absent as a breeding species in the British Isles, where there was concern about its passing as early as the sixteenth century.

The fishermen and explorers who reached primal America saw the fish hawk wherever they went, and the Indians had lived with this bird and presumably related themselves to it in many ways for thousands of years. Transmitted memories of the Osage Indians, for example, may indicate that they once regarded the osprey as a favored symbol, before they rejected it in favor of the swift and ruthless falcon, as more appropriate for the courage and endurance needed by a man and his tribe. J. J. Mathews, in *The Osages, Children of the Middle Waters*, writes:

"But there is evidence even so, that the Wah-Sha-She, the Water people, wanted to adopt the osprey, since he was of the water, really, and lived on fish. According to the modern Little Old Men, especially those of the Wah-Sha-She, they had liked the way in which the osprey splashed the surface of the water and came up with a fish, and the nervous fright he inspired among the others of the water. The grackles feeding on the margin of the lake, and the blue-winged teal feeding among the reeds would rise and circle in reconnaissance, and coots would run on the water, splashing their way into the air. The frogs leaped from their hunting stations and the turtles rolled off their logs. All this indicated the great importance of the osprey, but still he feared the bald eagle."

The Travels of William Bartram, 1791, mentions "the fishing hawk" as a "large bird, of high and rapid flight; his wings are very long and pointed, and he spreads a vast sail, in proportion to the width of his body. This princely bird subsists entirely on fish which he takes himself, scorning to live and grow fat on the dear-earned labor of another; he also contributes to the support of the bald eagle."

Perhaps this evolutionary sequence, in which it is forced to drop its fish in midair and have it stolen by the bald eagle, was never a matter of great concern to the osprey. There were always more fish to catch, and in any case chasing and stealing is common behavior, a part of the game, among a number of water bird species. But this particular behavioral link may become part of the lost archives division, since the bald eagle is approaching extinction in this country; and it may be that the osprey is going the same way.

Again we have the ability to destroy from a distance, and so we can rationalize ourselves out of context, often indeed almost out of sight. It seems astonishing that the old varied culture of the American Indian, which had an intimate, alive, spiritual connection with all nature on this continent should have almost completely vanished. Many Indians had the kind of knowledge of terrain, and the ability to find their way, which a modern urban man might call supernatural. Their ceremonial rounds were tied in with the giving and the taking away of the seasons, the dearth and abundance of crops and game. They identified with what they depended on, which may make them limited in our terms, and at the same time all the life of earth was available to them in their worship and the pride of worship. Each natural thing, whether an ant or an osprey, without any particular hierarchy among the animals, was considered to be a possible source of mystic power to any man, and they found celestial patrons in the stars.

Our range, our capability of action, has vastly increased over the Indians', and of course with the technology they had they could do no more damage than they did. They could make very little dent on their environment, and diseases were beyond their control. They set fires, but their effects were usually limited and not beyond restoration, which was the case of agricultural lands whose soil was impoverished through over-use. In short, conservation was not in the Indians' world at all.

Now, having replaced that balance, that spiritual intimacy thousands of years in the making, we have to take care, and is it care enough? Man's power to change his environment and everything in it may not only be overwhelming in its effects but so quick as to go unnoticed, a magic that deceived its own maker.

Not long ago, the osprey, which most people are unable to tell from a herring gull, even if it comes close enough to shoot, was still a relatively common sight along the northeast coast. Islands in Maine sheltered a large number of breeding pairs every year. Plymouth, Bristol and Barnstable counties in Massachusetts also had a big population. Their great nests, piled up on the tops of dead trees, or other eminences, high and low, were very evident in the Narragansett Bay region of Rhode Island and at the mouth of the Connecticut River, and the largest concentration of all was in Long Island, where over a thousand pair are reputed to have nested at one time, principally in the colonies at Gardiner's Island and Plum Island. There are now no ospreys left on Plum Island.

As with other species of American animals, there may have been a definite reduction in the breeding population of ospreys since colonial days, but they kept their numbers fairly well until some years after World War II, and then they began to decline at a rapid rate. An osprey nest count for Narragansett Bay shows 140 in the year 1949 being reduced to 33 by 1962, and since then the population graph shows a downward curve that is going out of sight. A study by Peter Ames of the breeding population of ospreys along the Connecticut River in Middlesex and New London counties, Connecticut, showed that they had decreased from about 200 pair in the early 1940s to 71 pair in 1960 and 24 in 1963. A 1964 count showed 15 pair. Subsequent figures for the Connecticut River area show that 14 pair nested in 1966, producing 5 young. In 1967, 11 pair nested, producing only 1 young; and at this writing there are 9 nests or 18 adults, with the outcome unknown. The vanishing point would seem to be in sight.

The same dismal process, in the same period of time, has been going on in Long Island, New York. Gardiner's Island used to have a fairly regular concentration of ospreys, with about 200 nests. Before 1957 all were healthily occupied in raising young, but since then reproduction has been poor. Although three or four hundred adults were there in the summer of 1966 many did not lay eggs at all. Others produced infertile eggs or hatched young birds which died early in the nest. Apparently not more than about 30 young were reared, compared to an annual output of 250 or more not too many years previously. Clearly, when the old birds die, there will soon be none left in Long Island, or Connecticut or Rhode Island, nor is the general picture a great deal better in the country as a whole, where ospreys are on the decline, if to varying degrees. There has been an alarming decline in the state of Michigan for example, but in parts of the south the fish hawks seem to have been maintaining their numbers in recent years. There are still fairly large breeding populations in Chesapeake Bay and on the Potomac River in which the numbers of adults have not markedly declined, but there is apparently some reason to believe that reproductive success may be on the downgrade there too.

In Canada, especially in those lakes and ponds not touched by "progress," the osprey seems to have been holding its own, but the recent news from there shows that progress is hard to confine. A government survey — and here the osprey's enemy is indicated — states that breeding populations of osprey and bald eagles once plentiful in the lakes of Ontario have begun to die out, because of the use of poison sprays. The peregrine falcon, the loon, and also fish, are included in the category of wildlife being killed off, or their reproductive capacity impaired, by the use of pesticides, especially "hard" ones like DDT.

Apparently what wanton use of firearms cannot do may be accomplished by the widespread application of insecticides, more particularly, those used against pests. Their murderous effects are still being investigated and it may take some time to prove them decisively enough to satisfy all hands, but one wonders how long we can afford to wait. The chlorinated hydrocarbons, such as DDT, DDE and derivatives of DDT, tend to accumulate in nature. They do not break down. They not only last in an environment but build up and magnify in its organic components. The original small, diluted concentrations of these chemicals tend to build up in a food chain so as to end in a concentration that may be thousands of times as strong. In a shore environment pesticides will begin to accumulate in plant life — the base of the energy structure in a natural community — and then they will become progressively more concentrated as they are passed on through plant eaters, insects, marine invertebrates and fish. The final victims are the carnivorous birds, such as fish-eating ducks, hawks, terns and herons which take the poison into their fatty tissues with compound interest.

These chemicals are carried far and wide. Particles of DDT sprayed by airplanes go into the atmosphere to be spread around the world, and runoff waters of all kinds, including rivers, streams, creeks and estuaries, carry them great distances after they have been used on the ground — they go into the earth-girdling currents of the seas. Even the Antarctic regions are not remote enough; DDT has been found in krill and in the bodies of fish and penguins. The damage such poisons have been causing the fragile and far-reaching ecological systems in nature is incalculable.

Most of the decline in ospreys has been associated

with the failure of eggs to hatch, though in some areas young birds have died before leaving the nest. Since DDT and DDE residues were found in osprey eggs in various regions, from Maine to Maryland, as well as in the fish the birds brought to their nests, they were long ago considered a very likely cause of infertile and unhatched eggs, not to mention sterility in the adults. It must be admitted that the decline of the osprey began, if slowly and gradually, a good many years ago. Ornithologists have been reporting a lessening of their numbers since the beginning of this century. On the other hand this decline was not precipitous until after World War II, with the wholesale spraying of pesticides. The coincidence comes close to appearing obvious. DDT rained on Long Island, for example, beginning in 1957. After that year osprey reproduction was markedly poor.

It is also possible that the interference of nesting gulls, now hugely increased in population, may have been a factor in suppressing the ospreys, as well as marinas, housing developments, the near and noisy presence of man and all his works. Nesting ospreys are often easily disturbed. In some areas, random shooting of the adults may have had serious effects. If one of a nesting pair is killed, the nest is likely to fail. But to say that human population and urban growth has a damaging effect must be balanced off against the fact that at one time ospreys used to nest on telephone poles along the busiest highways.

The magnitude of the osprey's decline is such that encroachment by human beings does not seem enough to account for it. It is pertinent that bald eagles which nested in remote areas in northern Minnesota where human disturbance could not be blamed for reproductive failure were no more successful in hatching eggs and rearing young than eagles nesting in regions that people could easily reach.

Some conscientious scientific workers, as well as the chemical industry (one for more disinterested reasons than the other), are still inclined to extreme caution when it comes to blaming the population decline of ospreys, and some other species, on pesticides. They do not find it susceptible of exact proof, or they say that there has not been time enough to find out. Under present circumstances, the latter statement sounds a little like asking us to wait another few generations to see how much effect radiation has on human genes. Where, in testing bombs or spraying, is the final proving ground?

Most people, short of swallowing DDT out of a tumbler, can agree to the fact that it is a poison, even in very diluted form, meant, after all, to kill. It is only the extent of the danger that lacks agreement, but it must be clear that that extent goes far and wide. We now know that o.6 to 6 parts per *billion* of DDT will kill off populations of shrimp in a couple of days. In addition, this pesticide has been found to markedly reduce the ability of marine plankton to photosynthesize; and since plankton is the massive, basic food of the sea, the implications are disturbing at the very least.

Anyone who has seen what may happen to birds some time after a town has sprayed its roadsides with a liberal dose of poison or a plane has gone overhead puffing it lazily into the atmosphere, must realize that these pitiful, dying animals, shaking with nerve spasms, have something to prove, even though their only way to be articulate about it is to die. One comes across these birds only on occasion. After all, the roads are often strewn with birds that have been hit by cars, and we may be slow to admit what happened to the others.

The fact is that the effects of our actions on the environment may be so widespread and above all so subtle as to nearly defy analysis. Mathematical proof is sometimes lacking simply because there can be no such thing. Also, we do not know at what time the great far-reaching, fluid processes of nature may be dangerously altered by our acts and changes simply because we cannot be aware of all of them at once. We are limited. We do not know why certain things happen as a result of our concoctions, our interference; we only know that they do happen, but we should not be so mesmerized by the unknown magnitude of this threat that we are unable to take any action.

We can no longer ignore the evidences against pesticides. No matter how much we hedge in the name of scientific proof, we must recognize that shrimp, plankton, fish, birds and even men (to a yet unexplored extent) have been destroyed, damaged, or impaired by hydrocarbons. It ought to be enough for us that breeding populations are dying out among ospreys and other species whose tissues have been found to be loaded with poisons. Lack of definitive evidence does not deny the obvious fact that there are any number of ways in which DDT might affect birds, at any time of the year, during any part of their cycle of breeding and migration. And one clear, scientific piece of evidence recently uncovered is that DDT affects the metabolic process whereby a bird metabolizes calcium, resulting in thin-shelled eggs. The bearing that a thin-shelled egg has on a chick's survival should be obvious.

Furthermore, in at least one area where restraint was used in the spraying of pesticides, the decline in a breeding population appears to have been arrested. After all the local agencies had agreed to a marked reduction in such use, starting in 1964, adult ospreys along the Westport River in Massachusetts not only held their numbers, but their nests suddenly began to be more productive. In the fifth successive year, the number of chicks hatched out and reared in proportion to the number of eggs laid had gone up from small percentages to 66 per cent. That seems to be at least one instance where reasonable proof is not lacking, and others should appear, and none too soon, as similar efforts are made, and studies pursued, with care and adequate support.

We once thought the earth was big enough, with its atmosphere, its rivers and its seas, to absorb anything we could do, but it is no longer capacious enough to dissipate our acts. They come back, around the world. Even the Eskimos have DDT in their tissues. The poisons we have already introduced into our environment, without adding any more, are enough to last for generations, and still we imperial innocents go on shaking them out with no more concern than if we were using a can of talcum powder. Not long ago it was discovered that one of the finest, protected salt marshes along the New England coast contained six pounds of DDT per square acre. After twenty years of spraying for mosquito control, salt marshes in Long Island were found to contain up to thirty-two pounds per acre.

The damage done is becoming more obvious every day, the facts grow more conclusive, and our apathy grows with them. Ordinarily a poisoner is put in the category of criminals. Should we except ourselves simply on the grounds that human beings are tougher than birds and that anyway we are not sure yet what the ultimate damage may be!

So when I looked at the wounded osprey, I saw a near ghost, or at least an old American now living in a world it never made, a symbol of old wilderness in a new one, man-created. What could it do in a society based on indifference toward it?

I had never seen an osprey up close before. My meetings with them had all been by chance, and I had rarely seen more than a pair at a time. As I sat on the beach at Cape Hatteras one spring, with the great breakers coming in from far out, line after line, plunging massively onto the sands, I saw an osprey as it flew in out of a tall, empty sky. It hovered over the shoreline like a great flower, its big rounded wings beating down, and the black and white colors showing bold and fine. Then a few herring gulls came in and then more osprey, five or six, and they all hovered and made wide circles over the waves. Then more gulls flew in and finally all the birds together went circling and sailing out over the sea like a slowly whirling cloud. It seemed to me that I had been given a new sense of the shore in all its proper scope.

I have also seen the fishing hawks along the coast of Maine where they fly steadily over the water between mist-belted islands, often with fish in their talons, or can be seen flapping and wheeling overhead. Once I saw an osprey over its nest, a big pile of material high up on a dead spruce; it was rising up, then plummeting down again within reach of its nest — where it undoubtedly had young — and wildly screaming. Later on I saw another fly in over an inlet when the tide was ebbing and the waters getting shallower. The great bird hovered, then dropped suddenly with wings partly bent, legs and feet straight down, and came up with a fish in its talons. After that it gave a shrill "Chip! Chip!" of triumph and flapped on measured wings into the distance.

The captive osprey had an oddly harum-scarum appearance, possibly because of the feathers on its black and white striped head, whch it lifted into an overall crest, and its light-orange eyes were set close together. Its wings, now sadly drooping, were very large, and the tips of their velvety, dark brown feathers had curved white edges. The bird's black, hooked beak was formidable, and its pale legs and black taloned feet stout and muscular. Its glowing eyes stared at me, with what mixture of nervous fear and pain, or mere consciousness of a fleeting existence, I could not start to guess. Having too serious a wound for anything but amputation, the osprey was "put away" not long after that, and I am still looking at a pair of wild, close-set eyes out of an Indian, American, indefinite world past, which those eyes knew *without* looking.

Out there over the free waters, the bird dove again, and screamed. A single dive, and success . . . and when I saw it my scalp tingled and I connected with the continental beauty of it; the act was like a hot iron plunged into the cold sea, and it joined the islands and water, fish and sky together.

Again, we live in a confusing labyrinth of human effects, which is one of the reasons why it is so hard for us to correct the damage we do. It may take a long time to find out how the fish hawk embryo was killed, to know which of a number of factors has decimated the population of inshore fish, to know where to go for an answer, or whom to ask. It is not only that we are now able to manipulate and change the environment, but a great displacement has occurred. Men are no longer complete dependents — except in the sense of being bound to their own actions. We have a new kind of freedom that constructs its own mirrors for the imagination; with it we form and transform matter on our own; but in freedom's name, under its auspices, we pollute and destroy in the most lazy and sordid way imaginable. Supposedly, we can "Improve on Nature"; but we are beginning to have less and less to improve on. Left to our own devices, after the osprey, the peregrine, the bald eagle and numerous other proud species are extinct, how, in the name of all the stars, are we going to be able to do better!

In spite of all our pretended substitutions, there is no substitute for a common respect for everything that has reached the distinction of life. The osprey is a power of its own, sacred to a million years. More men are needed who in thinking well of an osprey do not thereby think better of themselves.

IV

The Shape of Water

By this I found also that nothing that stood still, could by doing so be a part of Happiness, and that Affection, though it were invisible, were the best of Motions.

—Thomas Traherne

SUDDENLY, we have left behind the conquerable wilderness which forced us into a fighting and sometimes loving relationship with nature. Subsistence farming, the self-sufficient locality, the man with his own mountain or his own shore, are not to be depended on for guidance. So we are world-widers, and haphazard ones at that. Who was responsible for letting loose the insecticides? Well, I for one. When the spray cans came out on the open market with their solution to everything from the potato bug to the clothes moth, did I not have my shelves full of them? Who drives at high speed over crowded highways at the risk of his neck? Well, I cannot be self-denying about that.

Do I not accept the power, and the energy, the

mobility of the civilization on which I depend? I complain, yes, but I am a dependent, and I might even draw some excitement out of the idea of a new universality through knowledge and communication. But I am none too sure of the grounds on which I stand. How wise do I have to be to own pesticides, detergents, barbiturates, cars and guns, and how wise are they who provide me with them? The truth is that the possible consequences of my own ignorance, or idiocy, carried out on a global scale, stretched from the spray can to the hydrogen bomb, are almost too much for me to contemplate.

We alter, erase and poison the landscape at will, and sometimes, as in the case of the species of plants and animals we destroy, the results may go unnoticed. We ourselves are such wonderfully adaptable organisms that we hardly detect, let alone know how to identify, the damage, even when it affects our own bodies.

But the resources we are now claiming and using up at a reckless rate are not only our own. They belong to the whole earth, and to all other organisms that use the light of the sun, the water and the soil for their subsistence. Without these other lives we would not last long. We are creating a new and more terrible wilderness, not only for an osprey but ourselves. All our sustenance is not self-engendered. Man's cosmos naturally thrives on innovation and outwardness and it will starve on a diet of bread and water, doled out in its own crowded jail. Our capacity to adapt, which is a part of evolution, our place in all survival, still needs the freedom of earth as its companion.

There is a connection between man and the earth which is writ in water but has more depth than we give it credit for. I watch the waves along the shore for a force beyond exploitation, though I know we view the sea they come from as a commodity, like everything else. The oil drillers are after it. It is being used for wastes on a gigantic scale as we run out of room — or perhaps the intelligent ability — to dispose of them on land. The sea is being treated as a one remaining source of supply, but not as it used to be, a hardwon if terrible friend. Since we can fly over it in no time, that wide oceanic context is not as closely known as it was to the men in Melville's *Moby Dick*, for example, as they pursued their whales in open boats with the mother ship behind.

"It was a sight full of quick wonder and awe! The vast swells of the omnipotent sea; the surging, hollow roar they made, as they rolled along the eight gunwales, like gigantic bowls in a boundless bowling-green; the brief suspended agony of the boat, as it would tip for an instant on the knife-like edge of the sharper waves, that almost seemed threatening to cut it in two; the sudden profound dip into the watery glens and hollows; the keen spurrings and goadings to gain the top of the opposite hill; the headlong, sled-like slide down to its other side; — all these, with the cries of the headsmen and harpooners, and the shuddering gasps of the oarsmen, with the wondrous sight of the ivory *Pequod* bearing down upon her boats with outstretched sails, like a wild hen after her screaming brood."

The omnipotent landscape of the sea is something we have not been able to change or spoil, and its beauties go on rolling and re-forming under the wild sky in an alliance with all that surpasses history and all that makes it. This quality of depth and escape in the sea may yet hold us to a primitive relationship, one which is not entirely definable, as elusive as the waves themselves. A wave is primarily a shape, after all, a form in motion, traveling through water that scarcely moves as it passes; its water particles move in circles, so in a sense it rolls forward. Waves are of the water and at the same time something else, a fluid form of energy roving under the wind, and so allied to all weather, classic in form and at the same time multiformed, definable but continuous in too many ways to catch.

As I watch the small waves falling at my feet along the shore, I see measurement, consistency, the realm of order. In that, they are with the tides, the coming of the seasons, the unseen wave impulses in the air, which we adapt to our purposes as we can. Their measured alternations can be recorded by methods that are increasingly refined. The frequencies of storm waves moving over great distances can be checked by computers, those modern extensions of the mind which can look at our income tax forms or life statistics with a remote and unappeasable glance. Waves are a precise if complex aspect of exploitable energy.

Waves may not only correspond to such obvious outward phenomena as the seasons, but to those repeated rhythmic responses we find in our own behavior. What our timing, our order, or lapses from order, may mean is not always clear, but the wavelike impulses never leave us. Experience is made of waves. Our technology draws them, to its advantage, unseen out of the air. Our senses are only aware of an infinitesimal part of that universe of electromagnetic waves that surround us, pass us and go right through our bodies. To suggest equivalences between our emotions and the physical world may be risky, but there is no question that everything we do, whatever we say and how we say it, is in a context of recurrence like the waves.

Waves can be measured and recorded, and at the same time, like snowflakes, no two are alike. They vary from those gentle forms that lap against a canoe or the timbers of a wharf, to the giants out in the crossrunning, complicated surfaces of the sea. On a calm day you may see long, low swells coming in to the beach, one after another, hour after hour, under faint crisscrossed patterns made by local winds, and occasional patches, or cat's-paws, farther out under the veering and whisking of the breeze. Waves engendered in an unseen distance by a storm also come regularly over the sea, crossed over by locally generated waves that have a ghostly lightness. Waves crash into the shore as breakers, or fall in light, low forms along the beach with a sidelong, slipping motion, making an almost ripping or tearing sound on the sands. They join a landscape which is an integral part of that same compelling order, precise in every part, but in every part various enough so as to be ready for indefinite renewal. If I, a mere man, could claim as much I might guarantee the future of my race.

2

For a long time I have been going down to another landing on this long Atlantic shore. The road there meets a stretch of beach, cut through by an inlet, on Cape Cod Bay. Beach plum, wild cherry and beach grass cover the low dunes behind it. Over the years and the seasons its characteristic ingredients, sand, birds, clam worms, minnows or cloud fish in the sky have changed with the order of the environment, but their interplay has always been different, and it is this shifting, like the light on water lanes across the sandy flats, that has enticed me to continue on.

One day the sun lies hot and heavy on listless waters, while on another the light is weak, the air is cold, and an east wind drives stinging sand grains ahead of it and turns tidal waters into wide, shivering and stretching fields of action. On certain days in the fall the wind blows free and loose over the marshes behind the sea beach, sending cloud shadows like waves concurrently with shadows made by reddening marsh grasses and the heavy yellow heads of seaside goldenrod. The color-changes there, from green to red and yellow, from red and yellow to brown, become a matter more of riches struck into fire than dying down and routine change. The same wind roves wide and free over the bay's surfaces. When the tide is high the inshore waters are radiantly green where the sunlight hits them out of clouds, accented with whitecaps as fresh as the sanderlings suddenly shooting by in the brisk air, and, hatched and braided on their surfaces, they are a bright blue where they move into the inlet that joins beach to marsh. The sharp points of the cordgrasses bend, shiver, and glisten where they show through little waves.

This would be one day in the year; and a shore covered with cakes of ice as far as you can see would be part of another; and on most days there are shimmering wide flats at low tide, where all horizons seem opened up. Avenues and lanes of water lie in through ribbed sands stretching two or three miles out to the line marking the sea's retreat before the tide turns again, water that is pressured lightly and wrinkled by the wind, and flashes in the sunlight. The webbed feet of gulls leave cross-bow prints, and meandering tracks or holes are left by millions of sand-dwelling animals.

Offshore, in late spring or summer, terns dive for fish, great black-backed gulls stroke through the air with an accomplished dignity, growling hoarsely. Herring gulls sound in the distance down the beach, with almost bell-like cries. Crows move over tidal grounds like black leaves. Under clouds wind-drifted, shadows pass over glaring sands, whisking softly by at times, line after line, or moving lazily, sometimes tossing and swirling like leaves out of a bonfire, like the running lives in tidal waters, the ripples in the sand beneath.

Whenever I walk down to the beach, which is itself a product of wave action, I can see evidence of the waves in earth history, the measured intervals that roll forward from millions of years in the past. Glacial till shows it, or the grain of sand that was once a fragment of rock. Remnants of tree trunks now covered by the tide show that the shore has been cut away or inundated when it may no longer have been protected by an offshore bar. The gradual rise in sea level over past centuries can be measured by the depth of peat in the marshes, made by the saltwater cordgrass. And in the present, between the wavelike records of the past, is continuous action. The low waves and offshore currents move and mold the sand. They bend around the points and headlands and push back and forth between the sharp-pointed grasses. The structure of the shore is eloquent; from one curve and indentation to another it stands out strongly in its definitions. Each sandy bank, each jutting prow of peat and marsh grass, each rock, or varying levels at the water's edge, is an immediate influence as well as part of history, and it causes variations in the way the water meets it.

On some days the shore seems calm, compliant, restricted in dimension when the tide is in, while on others it springs with conflict and force. When the north wind blows, individual sand grains bounce across the asphalt of the parking lot, and sheets of them drive across the surface of the beach. At high or mid-tide the waters seem to run back and forth, seething with give-and-take, malleability and resistance. Wind strikes their surfaces, shifting and spreading them, cutting at them, turning and whipping. From the land's rim to where the waves slop on the horizon like water in a bucket, there is a wild stiffness and obstinacy, a northern energy at war with itself.

On other days I see all haze and illusion. The light over the flats on some September days distorts perspective so that a man coming toward you looks like an eight-foot giant. Way off in the hazy distance along the curving shore, cliffs and headlands show up as separated from each other across the water, isolated towers and islands swimming in the air. Waves coming up over the sandbar two miles away look like low-flying shapes. Groups of people at that distance, or the ever-present community of gulls standing into the wind, become either outsized or dematerialized. Reality becomes a mirage.

The tidal flats as a vantage point on the globe have more open space than most. They are full of storm tossings, regularity, the constant influences of world weather, beauties of reflection, changes in mood. Sometimes, as on autumn days, they summon you out of an evanescence joined with the whole sky. Their volatility is open to our own, even those waves of emotion which may not fly loose over a sandbar, or be useful to investigation, but are of nature and her sea sure enough. They invite me to an extension of myself, with no divisions of matter or spirit. Even my inner turmoil may be a measure of my hope to find.

The wavelets bob and move in shallow water as the tide comes in, and the sands stir as old ripple marks are reshaped and new ones made. Wind, the pressure of air, starts the classic wave in motion. The wave itself shapes the sand beneath it, but each medium, water or air, has its separate laws and conditions. When I first started looking at ripples with idle interest, I took it for granted that they ran parallel to each other, which may be correct to some degree, and I also thought — in our habits of looking for sameness in things — that the mechanics of their formation over dry, blown sand was the same as it is over its tidal floats, which is not the case. Ripple marks caused by water are irregular in shape, consisting of separate hillocks, shelving curves and pockets which have no particular tendency to run transverse to the direction of the water's flow. Over the wide flats they have a variety of shapes in different places, teeth, wedges, almost stonelike patterns curled and bobbed. There are long curved ripples with regularly shaped troughs, and short divided ones. They reflect the water over them, its rocking back and forth under the wavelets running in and back with the tides. In other words their shapes are made by the oscillation of water. If you watch fine, even sand as wavelets begin to move back and forth over it, you can see a process whereby the troughs and crests of ripples are made. If there is the slightest indentation in the sand the backward pull of the water enlarges it while some of the sand taken from it is deposited on the crest above, then the crest and trough seems to be redefined when the water flows forward again.

Ripple forming, in terms of the relative force of the waves and currents and the physical nature of the sand, is a changing and often complex process. On an incoming tide, on a windy day, the advance wavelets move back and forth — with their own complex interrelationship — defining and redefining the shape of troughs and crests beneath them, while the large waves just behind them continually sweep in and break, having their own effect on the bottom. The wavelets in their forward motion make ripples that have long slopes on the seaward side, short steep fronts on the other; and then as they wash back they temporarily redefine these ripples, making a thin edge on their top, then a flat plateau. When the tide is finally in, or out, the ripples may in general have this characteristic shape, with a long slope on one side and a steep one on the other, but just as often they represent a kind of balance of moldings made by the water. To watch their making is to participate in continual motion; their form can be explained, it may be momentarily fixed, but it is never final.

There is a great deal more free motion in the air than there is in water. Apparently the ripples of a dune, desert, or dry beach are the result of repeated impact by sand grains on the surface as they are bounced forward by the wind in close proximity. In the heavier, buoyant medium of the water, on the other hand, sand grains are being lifted and moved individually, and only strike the bottom feebly. The distance each grain travels has nothing to do with the general shape of the ripples formed by the mass of grains, whereas the length and shape of a ripple formed by air is the result of the repeated travel and piling up of sand grains over average distances.

So with these few definitions partly understood, and in ignorance of many more, I have spent hours watching the tide flood and ebb, with an unfinished fascination at all the sand patterns in the making, remaking, or being left behind. This is water work, from the sea wave to the wavelet, out of depths into shallows, part of its vortexes and eddies, its inter-rushing and meeting . . . too much to catch. I am bound to be late, in this sea range where the water toward the north works the horizon and is worked on by the light, comes and receives all coming. The distance slips and ravages. Time and calculation move in a flood where we are left behind. With what ferocity we hang on to what we can get, to what little we can do! Still, the salty hour, the pulse, the immediate apprehension of these fleeting things, remain. There is a correspondence in us to those regular but indefinite motions of water and light spreading off over the curvature of the globe. Life allies us to a current that invites all distances.

V

In Front of the Sea

JUST so long as there is a wildness to find I can stay alive. It is not that I want it for an escape, since that is impossible in this world, but to share. The exchange of life is what is important. Unless we can see the "non-human" environment in terms of a whole that only acts, gives and receives fully when all its elements are in full play, then we will still be on the outside looking in. It may be that what we need more than anything else is to shake hands with the "insignificant."

Returning to the flats one day and trying to understand how the orbital motion of the water made ripples, I caught sight of a very small surf clam, lying on the surface. Five minutes later I saw it quickly flip over, slice into the sand edgewise, its anterior end first, and disappear, all in a matter of seconds. To have what I thought of as an inanimate, rudimentary object act like that startled me. It leaped into life. Clams, to those who have studied them with any care,

are of course feeding, breathing, digesting, reproducing organisms. One biologist remarked that he knew too much about clams to be able to eat them. But to those of us who may think of them either as seashells or edible commodities, their status as living entities is apt to be low. That quick flip into the sands made me realize that I was in the presence of something else that not only deserved attention but added to the place where it existed. At least I was unable to say: "There's nothing here but a clam."

Of course the clam, in this wide, rippled wilderness, coexists with scavengers and carnivores, suspension feeders and deposit feeders. All of them depend on sea water. Most of them have to have a tremendous reproductive potential to keep up with great mortality. These animals, living and dying by the million, need a commensurate amount of food. The minute organisms in salt water, thousands or millions in a cubic yard, consumed by mussels, barnacles, worms or clams, provide the basic nourishment of the shore. And in this environment the clam or shrimp fights for survival, to feed and to increase in a range favorable to it, whether muddy, sandy, at low or high tide level. Even ripples play a part. When they occur in very pronounced form, ripples may keep out some populations of inshore marine animals because they are evidence of unstable sediment, caused by turbulence, in which some organisms are unable to thrive. Sandy surfaces that smooth out during the summer when

shallow tidal areas are calmer tend to encourage the
growth of diatoms, which is accompanied by a growth
of various kinds of sea worms and molluscs which
feed on them. And these animals, living in various
areas with various conditions of mud or sand, or a
combination of both, are in competition for the available food. The presence of a large number of one kind
may keep others away. There is one tiny clam, light
purple in color like the inside of a quahog, called
Gemma gemma. Myriads of their dead shells may line
the troughs of the ripple marks or be mixed through
the open flats but go unnoticed unless you pick up a
handful of sand. But with a hand glass the shell comes
to sight in all its color and delicacy. This clam, by the
way, is ovoviparous. Its young are hatched inside it;
and when freed into the water they settle around their
parent, not a warm relationship necessarily, but close
enough.

Studies have indicated that populations of Gem-
mas, tiny as the individuals are, can seriously mo-
nopolize an area, keeping other feeding animals out.
Many thousands, each siphoning in the seawater and
filtering the food particles from it, can take a large
proportion of the available local food. Larvae of soft-
shell clams, for example, that landed in such a dense
Gemma-dominated environment would not have much
chance of surviving. It seems that size is no proof of
strength.

The signatories of other millions that lie under the

surface are almost everywhere. Raised trails, indented tracks, mounds or holes, indicate great and active populations, although a first look at the flats may give you the impression of a desert. I suppose that most of us begin by looking out from the mold of our needs and see what we want to see. A bather sees sun and water. The clam diggers and the fisheries biologists who are primarily concerned with the propagation of hard and soft-shelled clams see only them when they face the flats. The pressure of the tiny ones, like *Gemma gemma*, which may keep the edible clam from generating, are seldom noticed, though the large horseshoe crab, which is, and feeds in part on young clams, suffers the consequences. In some regions this antediluvian and in many ways fascinating animal is dying out through too active persecution — and there is no other term for it.

In spite of their surface signs, these water-woven plains are not easily resolved into the specific lives they hold without some trained attention. They make a remote environment, their surfaces always shifted lightly by the elements, and sometimes drastically, as in a storm, or by human agency, when marshes are filled in, inlets torn up, breakwaters and jetties constantly built so as to save beaches their forerunners may have seriously altered. They move and change and whatever lives may be reacting to their motion are largely hidden, except for the shorebirds that bob in the shallows or, from their dance of a flight, swing down to probe across the sands.

I may be able to assure myself, when walking through fields or woods, that I am in places where, as a land mammal, I can communicate with the inhabitants. I can also ally myself, anthropomorphically, with a thrush, a lightning-scorched tree, the prolific grasses, or almost anything else I meet, but the flats, in their primal flatness, their transparencies, their elusive organisms, seem in some respects like the surface of another planet. This is a foreign shore, except for whatever food gathering makes it familiar to me. I do not know a tenth of the inhabitants or how they live, eat and reproduce, or what their strange anatomies may mean. Some of them seem to have their hearts in their feet and their stomachs where their mouths ought to be. But it is very evident that what they are all obligated to is a standard of endurance so far as the world's shore environment is concerned. They live in regions of shallow water where there may be the most extreme variation in temperature over the year. Their greatest danger is desiccation when the flats are uncovered by the tide. They also have to survive storm waves, ice and heat, sudden shifts in the surface volumes of sand and mud which may bury them. For these burying little animals with twinkling legs, for these worms and crabs, life is drastic, pared down to essentials. They are closely allied with whatever bare principles in the universe call for the dignity of obedience.

I know, in spite of our scientific studies of its habits and nervous system, that a worm is still generally thought of as "only a worm." Also, in spite of the beauty which many of them do exhibit, there may be something about a merely eating and regenerating animal with sand grains in its gut which is both remote and terrifying. The sand grains provide appropriate spaces, the seawater brings in its food, and that is that . . . a life alone with elemental provision.

But someday I may take up the study of worms to prove how well they thread the world together.

2

ALMOST daily, the year around, people drive down to the landing above the flats, and there they park, to watch the sunset, or to make love, to drink or quarrel. There they sit in their cars and just look out toward the horizon, watching for ships and birds, or nothing at all. It is a going-out they come for, to act out fragments of their lives as neighbors under a sky which might allow them to, without a wall. This is a primal arena, simply accepted as such by everyone who goes there. They are there to occupy an openness that is waiting for them. In a sense they are there with the shorebirds, watching on the edges, ready to settle in on the sands.

I wonder if we do not feel invited to this open landscape not only because it soothes us but because we need it. Is there still a residual earth man inside us that looks to a wilderness where all his reactions fit and where it is natural to meet existence directly, with no artificial aid, no go-betweens?

This environment not only invites us to sunbathing and gathering shells and pebbles on the beach; it is a junction of several worlds, a meeting place. It has something of the stable power of the land, something of the wide, procreant wash of the sea. Inshore you can see unexpected, spontaneous events in response to the changing year, like the swarming of sand eels in the spring. The drama of the sea comes in with the freshwater herring that make their inland migration up the estuaries and freshwater creeks. In the summer there are minute organisms that cause the offshore waters to sparkle in the dark. In spring, late summer, fall, and the end of winter the birds weave sky, water and sands together with their migrations. Beyond the life of the shore is the exceptional vitality of a killer whale, of a school of mackerel or bluefish, and the marine depths that made them also bring in the plankton-bloom to color the waters and nourish the minnows that feed the terns. We see the order that brings these lives out to universal use in their timing, close to the timing of the year, in the temperatures of the water, in the motions, depths and currents of the sea. We see incomparable energy in their reproduction, sowing the future with their seed, in their savage takings, and in their major mortalities.

The whole earth shares in the provisions of such energy, and so does human history. Even to say that the life of man is brutal and short, that disaster is always in the cards, that war is an extension of the human condition, is in part to recognize a history which shares a terrible rapacity with the rest of nature. The truth is that we too, along with the bluefish, were originally endowed with a ferocity. Each man means a sending on, an intent to pass a barrier, and his failure to pass it is a potential cause of war. At the same time, since it is in us to leap like fish — half silvered with light, half made of darkness — we try, across failure and chaos, to express, not only the inexpressible, but whatever of these quantities and delicacies, fragile forms and drownings are met with in ourselves.

As a game, though, the theme has its lightness. I go down to the landing and I walk out on the sands simply because it is in me to move, like a hermit crab issuing tentatively from its borrowed shell. This little animal, to continue the shaky human analogy, may well be looking for a fight when it pokes out its claws and head. There is nothing it likes so much as to pick on its neighbors. Of course, when they move out of their shells, they have to do so in a hurry because of their soft bodies, or risk providing another crab with an easy meal. All this extending of stalked popeyes, the quick pulling out, the tentative forays, the fights between them, makes hermit crabs very entertaining; in fact why be too serious ourselves — when it comes to shells are we not quick-change artists too?

Human society itself is a form of game, a means not only of fitting to the earth environment but of moving back and forth with relation to it. In one sense or another we keep bouncing the ball against the back wall, as if continually looking for an opening, a strike, a gain. And it is the same way, surely, with all other organisms, although their curiosity, which is a part of play, is far more elaborated in us, to the extent that if the wall gets too frustrating we can try to make it disappear, although we risk the game. But surely we are still obligated to those depths that compel us to play, to exercise our hopes for fulfillment, to move toward all kinds of diversity of touch and exploration. It is not only our own frustration that leads to the wish for an open world.

3

Across the windy horizon Atlantic migrations meet and pass. During spring and fall the great arrivals and departures of sea and shorebirds take place, and in winter the offshore waters are full of black ducks, scoters and geese. At all times of the year gulls crowd the reaching sands, or flock across the water at high tide. They have a distinct tribal order of their own and perhaps more adaptability than most. They have such a talent at seizing their opportunity, taking advantage of all the food they can get, that they have increased their population at almost as fast a rate as our own. If food on the flats fails them then they can fly inland to the dumps or out to sea to follow the trawlers. It is as if they stood there on the human garbage wagon, keeping a wary eye on the driver. Sometimes when they pick up schools of fish in shallow waters there is a great chase among them and a wild, scrambled crowd crying lifts up, rasping, trembling screams that slide down into trills and mutterings, cries that sometimes sound like general protest, wailing and bitter greed.

What I see over the flats is not simply the flight of birds, or the arrival of fish, but a demonstration of standards, a revelation of use, which may mean opportunity for the herring gull, or the automatic putting out of siphons for food which is characteristic of a clam. In any case, action is specific to place and adds to its dimension.

I remember one windy October day when the whole seafront before me seemed brought together by wings. The flats were covered at high tide. The gull-gray clouds were roaming overhead and shafts of sunlight struck down through their openings. The greenish gray waters to seaward had a rocklike magnificence, lined with foam under the shock and tugging of the north wind. Inshore, the yellowing, wet marsh grasses speared up through waters that roiled and foamed, agitated and hurried on.

In shivering flight, flocks of brant geese came in from far out, and gannets, with ermine-white, black-tipped wings — that have a spread of six feet —

flapped and soared several miles off over the bay. They would wheel in bold and easy sweeps, with the sunlight shining on the brilliant whiteness of their feathers, and then plummet down with half-closed wings, and even at that distance I could see the spray they made on impact. Black ducks slanted up in quick flights and sped away. Mergansers flew like spearheads through the wind. A flock of terns circled together as its individual members dove into the surface waters after fish, like a moving cloud of snow, while others of these lithe, strong-winged sea swallows flew tensely and surely along the shoreline, beating up to windward. And under the wind the sanderlings went trippingly down the water's edge and moved in quick, short flights from one part of the beach to another.

The gannets loped and swung. The black-back and herring gulls flew into the wind with a slow, measured pace, as taut and rhythmic in their way as the waters spread out below them. The sea range rode with the wind, and even a watcher had to do some pitching and diving in himself, to rise up and hurry ahead, to wing over and settle down, to meet the shocks of air or avoid them.

4

ONE September I had an unexpected meeting with a shorebird. It was sitting at the end of a rock jetty that extended from the beach. Since the tide was high, the water kept lapping over the bird's feet, so that it hopped away occasionally, but without much concern. I identified it, because of a brownish red patch on its shoulders, as a western sandpiper, a rare visitor. These birds breed in coastal Alaska and their principle migrations occur along the Pacific coast, but a few make their way across the continent, to appear from Massachusetts southward. That bit of information gave this sandpiper a distinction in my sight, but its real proximity took it out of my field guide for good.

I only sat ten feet or so away from the bird. Perhaps it was tired after a long migratory flight. It stood on one leg, the other tucked in hard to its breast feathers, a partly locked-in position, I supposed, since it moved the leg out with a jerk after a while. Then it stood on its two legs and tucked its black down-curved bill into its back feathers, one little black eye open and watching me.

So there it was, out of a great distance, spanning a continent, in weariness, in temporary rest, preparedness. It had a life to show me, rare and ready. What more could I ask for in a meeting?

We ask what things are called, of what use they are, and what they do, as if the naming and function were everything. At this social distance other living things become facts, to be put down and filed away in our endless catalogues. So it was good to meet a western sandpiper, eye to eye. It satisfied a vital ignorance in me, an unexplored connection.

During the late summer and early autumn I very often see adult and young terns together on these sandy rims of the Cape. Before they migrate south, the parent birds are still feeding the young, which wait passively on the ground or take after their parents into the air. Terns fish for sand eels or silverside minnows, glistening little fish that the adults give to their young. Or they refuse them often enough so that by constant practice the young birds begin to fish fairly adeptly for themselves. It is a lesson of hard survival, on the edge of a season's turning, which has to be learned as these quick and excitable seabirds start their long journey south, though even then the young ones may be begging for food. They beat up into the wind like their elders, and they dive, often fruitlessly, into the shallows after fish, and they complain harshly, incessantly, as they beg for food. Their trying is so vital; there is such urgency in them! How is *any* life to express the little time allowed for learning and accomplishment?

The silvery fish that dangle from their slender bills are a central image and reality from the time they are nestlings to when they can feed for themselves. A tern uses fish in feeding its young, in courtship flights, in giving and withholding with its mate. The fish is the primal food, and it means survival on a primitive and symbolic — but why "non-human"? — level. Are we not part symbolists, part survivors too?

Wherever I go in these as yet "unimproved" areas, I get an invitation to see. The flats are full of specifics, hard order, precise reaction, between the interstices of sand and the eye of a bird that stalks above them. I often see yellowlegs close inshore between the salt-water grasses, or hear their fine-pitched whistle. They bob back and forth on long, slender legs and pivot around when chasing food in a shallow pool. They teeter and turn. They stretch out a long leg behind them with deliberate grace, wonderfully particular in motion. Just before flying off, if there are a number together, they act a little like ponies getting ready to run, bobbing and walking away together in the water. At the same time they move in semicircles around each other. Once I saw two yellowlegs, one circling completely around the other before they both flew off, for orientation perhaps, the second being the pivot or fulcrum of the two. With their delicate gray and brown feathering, black bills, long yellow legs, they go about their teetering and turning, their picking up food from shallow water, and yanking back and forth, mud-probing where the water is deeper, as if they were engaged in a dance.

When I meet the yellowlegs, I meet a natural delicacy and aptitude of a unique kind, but one which is ready in the balance of everything it meets. So, in a sense, these birds tell me not to stop with them.

One of the most common inhabitants of these coastal, inshore waters is the killifish, or mummichog, whose yellow-green, striped, somewhat dumpy bodies flit everywhere through sun-braided water over rippled sands. I had never paid them much attention until one day when I saw a tern dipping into the water over hundreds of killifish, back and forth, almost idly, as if it were looking for a species it liked better. Each time the tern dipped toward them they all rushed forward in a body.

Then I noticed — this was in mid-September — that the larger killifish were farther out and the little ones closer inshore, where there was less wave action, and presumably fewer predators. There were also some sand shrimp flicking quickly over the bottom which occasionally bumped my bare feet. There were two people wading in the vicinity who found killifish and shrimp thoroughly alarming. These quick little animals "hit" them and were ready to "grab" them. They were scared by all other possibilities, the crabs that bite, the stones that cut, the old weed-shrouded timbers of a wrecked ship that reminded them of hard luck and doomed lives. They picked their way gingerly out of there as if they were going through a dark alley. Perhaps they were. I can't boast of my superior attentiveness.

I noticed that the members of this killifish multitude, now part of all danger, had pebbly white dots on their backs, as do the nearly transparent, though grainy-backed, shrimp. These markings were integral with the easing, scintillating environment of summer sands, the water and the sunlight. They were almost exact counterparts of the shadow dots made on the bottom by sand grains floating on the surface. Where they swung easily over the sand, the killifish and their shadows appeared like double exposures. Their white bellies flashed in the light where they pushed into the sands, occasionally flipping along sideways, feeding there. In fact there were areas in which multitudes were nuzzling in the sand at once, sometimes making fair-sized pockets in it. Individuals would take sand in their mouths with whatever bits of food, small larvae or crustaceans it had in it, and then spit the grains out.

So they were traveling everywhere around me, threading patches of eelgrass like birds through tree branches or deer in a forest, flitting over the sand or flipping along its surface. Sand grains and bubbles moved with them, making a galaxy of reflections. The quiet tide had turned without my noticing. The stems of eelgrass and the lodged seaweeds were rolled over in the water so that they now pointed toward the shore. Overhead there were a few big cumulus clouds in a burning, pale sky, and higher cirrus like milk-weed floss, fine, long, many-layered skeins of silk. And I made for the dark shore and its depths and sounds, having come by these small steps toward another wideness and a few of its definitions. The killifish might only mean rapacity, the short season of a life, the cruelty of a beauty with which little things are endowed, a vanishing and a shadow, and still they said "come on."

VI

The Winter Strength

VIOLENCE and danger play a part in any natural landscape, however tame and stable it may seem. Decidedly, it is not out of place to wander across these flats in a half-frightened state at the things that sink into the sand so abruptly or may jump up and bite at any moment. It is not our exclusive environment in the first place; but perhaps we are even further removed from it. We bring our own violence with us, disguised as security. To play safe means to be dutiful to all those means by which men can enclose themselves within their speed, the amenities of their culture, their status in the community, and above all, their supreme ability to annihilate the opposition. Step outside those bounds and you are a mere clam worm and lose your face.

I recognize that the problem is not quite so simple as that. Most men are just as bewildered by their special human place in the universe, keeping them apart from the rest of nature, as they are afraid of losing it. But where on earth did fear itself originate? Perhaps we are ashamed that our hearts sometimes beat as fast as a rabbit's, but it is common enough, and even desirable. All those motivations we seem unable to control, all our unwanted inner conflict, our pain and our loss, provide experience with half its validity. Hate and love, also, have their own runs to make, following a logic which is as wide in its application, as little imposed, as the action of a storm or the light on the waves.

What we obey out of our own depths is not confined within optimistic predictions about our health or our economy. The force of having lived through unpredicted outcomes is what survival implies. We are of earth's universality and have to play life out in its awful terms; and still, we approach it like strangers who know better.

We meet nature's major, damaging constructions, hurricanes, drought, or ice storms, not in communality so much, to fight them or to hide, but as if they were sent to emphasize our difference. Some day, we assume, we will be their lion tamers, though everything tells us to take care. The consequences of trying to get rid of all the mosquitoes may be no less incalculable than trying to change and control the weather. How much abstraction can we assume and still be conquerors?

Strangely enough, part of this abstraction now goes along with the proliferation of things known. The extension of knowledge is such that no man on earth is unaffected by it, in terms of distance, in terms of the properties of matter, in terms of biologic action and motivation, of the inherent characteristics of all life species, endlessly, relentlessly analyzed. But along with applied science, applied indifference remains. It becomes harder to connect humanly, whole-heartedly. We may go down to the shore and identify, but neither identification nor our ability to systematize is any guarantee that we will move openly, expectantly toward what we find.

We have long cultivated the habit of thinking of the earth environment as having no meaning or application but what we give it. This cuts the earth down to a flat which has no bird tracks, or wormholes in it at all. The so called conquest of nature, which was made possible by nature's primal capacity to renew and provide, has almost put the human species on its own, a state of affairs which is getting us into more trouble every day. To draw on all the earth's resources without being able to give anything back is not an imbalance we could survive forever.

We may find too, that to go on discriminating between the earth's organisms in terms of economic convenience, and bad or good, useful or useless, will result in our eliminating all we need to hold our environment together. The haphazard, take-it-as-it-comes method of changing our habitat no longer works. We do not now change so much as overwhelm. And much that is essential to any environment — forest, tundra or shore — may be hidden to us in the first place. The earth requires cooperation from a vast number of interrelated organisms, from the invisible to what is available to our unaided eyes. We cannot remove the parts of nature's systems of communication without the greatest care. We have hardly begun to know how they work. We are reducing our own range of choice partly without knowing it. At least, we do not seem to take science's fair-minded view of things. We are more inclined to take our marching orders — like an army of ants — from rampant technology. We are all too quick at losing the memory of what we have just consumed and left behind!

Our reduction of the multifarious parts of the landscape means a reduction in revelation for ourselves. Surely we are in need of all the variousness earth can show us. The texture of life grows with association, and not just with your own kind. Vision or blind touch are as incomparable in the rest of creation as they are in us. These lower lives over which we walk are not just part of some ancient dispensation which we can replace with our own. They are part of the wide and continuing energy of the present. They express, in their various sensitive ways, the interdependence of the earth and what it offers, what it does and says to us. I do not have any reason to believe that I am more limited than anyone else in our violent and knowledgeable society simply because I always find, or expect to find, some education in merely meeting up with "these others." A hawk is the embodiment of a beauty which reaches to a man. When a fish swims I find an unused swimmer in me. Except as knowledge helps me, I do not expect to offer anything brand new to what is before me, but I hope to be ready to receive.

So far as context is concerned, I do not think that a trumpet worm, for example, living in its carefully made tube of golden sand grains in the salty flats, is any less or more artificial than a man in a city tower.

The lines go out, infinite analogies are possible, the earth spins and recombines its forces, within the never completely defined cosmic order. Each success in human definition leads to another corner around which we have to define again, a spur both to vision and despair. Behind appearances, the city of man, the city of the ant, the flower and the weather, natural energy keeps burning, and whether or not it may eventually run down through heat loss in the universe is a theory that should not bear too much on our present responsibility, which is dire enough.

To see the weather, or anything else in nature, only in terms of the human mastery of inconvenience, seems to me to apply human limitations where they do not belong. It is not honest to reality. Each to its cold, each to its heat. Try and turn the world thermostat up to a universal 70 degrees and you invite retaliation. The seasons, or thousands of years of geologic change, represent a majestic fluency whose ends we cannot even predict with much conviction, let alone control.

Even those restrictive winter days which encourage our complaints can serve as unsuspected measures of health and variety if we learn to let them in on their own terms. Hanging over land and sea, the clouds change and invite, with unchanging capacity to show us more than we knew existed. On some December days, the still breaking out, lunging days, halfway between an old warmth and a new extreme of cold, banks of white mountainous clouds lie over a dark, rough sea, giving the effect of an implanted mystery, with enormous caves to enter in. There is a cold, ponderous insistence in the high, sweeping air. The waters roar and spread out bluish-purple toward the horizon, green under an occasional down-striking shaft of sunlight. Then these great rolling, round, lighted clouds move inland driven by the wind. A gray cover spreads overhead and spits out snow showers between the trees, not just as dead crystals, cold effigies, beautiful constructions, but exhilarating, procreative, dancing and darting while the gnarled, twisted gray and black trees, standing in silence and fortitude, rock stiffly and zigzag down in patient lines as counterpoints to the wind and the snow siftings swept around them.

The winter from which I retreat brings me world forces massing for assault. When it is 43 below zero in Minnesota, 12 below in Chicago, when snow showers, then rain, and snow again, drive along the coastline spattering and ticking on the widows, an earth power flies at my face. The reality and place of rocking trees is returned to me, out of a world reemphasized, given its dimension. Down by the shore there is a wall of cold over the dark sand and the tide pools where the wind tries to split my skin. Beyond gray, riffled waters and silvery seaward light, beyond breathing and thunder over a sand bar three miles out, a cold and excellent enterprise builds another high wall, another example not to be imitated, moving away even as I approach it.

2

WINTER is not the bad season as opposed to spring, but both are full of momentous, sometimes cataclysmic happenings about which we will learn very little if we assume too much. Every minute the seasons hang in the balance, every minute they are transformed, like the wet snowball I hold in my hand, from which the water drips when I clench my fist. In that there is heat and cold, evaporation, the change of water from one state to another, all measurable and also part of a magnificent extension of energy that I hardly begin to realize. Am I not transformed myself through the touch of snow, the weight of the atmosphere? I am unable to take full advantage of it. There is a helpless rigidity in me, my saving identity, and its limitations. No one knows their capacity to change. But we are no more separated from universal force than our lungs are from the air we breathe. The transmutations of energy give us joy or make us cry, although we do not necessarily see it that way. Our systematics have to be joined by the sense of experience. What does it mean to know that freezing water exerts a pressure of 15 tons to the square inch, or that a storm wave's pressure may amount to several thousand tons per square foot? The ice and the ocean, the wave and the mountain, the air above us, withhold their immense weight and we take them for granted. I do not often have to consider the weight of the atmosphere on my body, unless I climb a mountain or walk out into a hurricane. I only realize the problem I have in standing up after I fall down. But it is to the measure of these great containments that we are sent ahead.

There is nothing in nature which is not some other manifestation of that incredible energy. It shines out in the wild flower as it does in our terrible and unexpected discoveries, but in nature's successes, its complete identities, there is also a precious momentum for any man. I see a tiny dark snow flea creeping slowly over crystals of packed snow. A sudden flick, a mighty leap, and it goes. What realm does it occupy? Where in my experience has such a meeting ever taken place before? I am on the outside looking in, but the flea wakes me up, to another legitimacy, a new proportion.

If man were a total outsider with respect to nature, how could he claim so much? Even ownership makes us part of what we claim, either for enrichment or destruction. I would include the flea for the sake of honesty. The mystery innate in it, its furtherness, is not found in the mere impetus of our age, but will outlast us all.

A new storm roars in with savage and strong winds. The Atlantic's green water is brown with churned-up sand along the shore. Waves spurt up under the lashing of the freezing air. Trial is here again. Every life that is not able to protect itself through some form of dormancy has to race through the air, shiver, crouch down or lie low. Under the cover of wind-drifted snow are lives bound to pitiless necessity. Along a marsh periphery under drifted piles of thatch, or under driftwood lying in sandy areas toward the shore, the meadow mice have their tunnels where they scurry and squeak. In one place a fox has tried to dig them out, leaving piles of sand at the rim of a heavy plank, and when I lift it, there under sand and beach grass is a grassy nest in one corner with burrows leading away from it. Even in winter, mice thrive on the plant life in these salt marsh areas and if mortality did not keep up with their prolific natures, they might overrun the earth. There may be something pitiable about these quivering little animals that have to supply a predatory world. On the other hand the provision for mice themselves transcends human sympathy. Grim isolation is not so much the characteristic of living communities as we might be inclined to think; the opposite is more likely, and in fact, their guarantee. Because they play a central role in the predator-prey relationship, great numbers of these mice are needed; but another way to put it is that great numbers of these mice are needed because they thrive by association, even with their predators. The more elaborate and widely connected an organic system is the more chances for health and stability. Nature needs the interplay of many lives and many species for its world to evolve with continual, open-ended success.

The winter season, in this relatively mild maritime climate, swings back and forth. Ice forms on rocks covered by the tides and on the surface of shallow inshore waters when the temperatures are consistently low enough to freeze salt water. A slushy ice forms in the water, gently rocked back and forth, a mass that moves with an almost rotary motion on an ebb tide, making a low seething sound. When the tide comes back it packs the ice up against the shore of coves and bays. White ice cakes gather on marshes too, lifted there or taken away by the tides. The ice saws and scrapes over stubs of saltwater grass and on warm days, days of gray and humid shadows, the water from melting ice trickles audibly underneath it. Ice, like snow, in all its various degrees of hardness, its texture sometimes crystalline and clear, sometimes crumbly and flaky, is a standard by which to measure the rhythm of these days.

Inland over marshes and into the thickets and trees, the tight twigs against the sky, the birds appear and disappear in fast, low flights. A white-throated sparrow flits up and down briskly, sparrow-fashion, between the yellow stalks of the summer's reeds and cattails, so definite in its brown feathers, quick and alert. This dash of a bird across my sight gives me a winged alliance, the living fact of a race that lives between one height of energy and another, in many parts of a continent. My nation, as well as the circumstances of my life, seems to shift and circle like sea ice, lagging and ponderous, and I do not see my way out, until the sparrow lifts me by its quickness.

And in the winter scheme of things there are days that seem to be made of a nearly indestructible symmetry. I know it to be in transition, but the landscape is so pure and precise, so bold and ironclad, as to invite me into a clean depth of its own. At low tide, and in the late afternoon, the offshore waters are bright blue, pushing in pack ice so that the distance is filled with a swishing roar, while along the beach is a hush, a winter silence. The sun is as bright and cool as glass, and begins to move down into horizons of smoky, flaring clouds, dull fires over distant, winter prairies in the sky. And toward the east there is a very large white moon, like the round seed head of a dandelion.

Crows stalk along the scalloped shore. A flock of brant probes in open tide pools and shallows not covered by ice. Two black ducks whir straight up, showing the whitish-silver feathers under their wings, quacking deeply. Several flocks of Canada geese, with bowed necks and great wings beating, bugle along the shore line.

The ripple patterns in the semifrozen sand are thicker and heavier than in the summertime, with squared off fronts, like shelving chunks of split wood, or with chainlike patterns. Boulders are capped with white ice, and ice cakes are distributed over the shore's dark sands like great dishes, gleaming in the light. Pools of open water change to pale green in the later afternoon and they are bordered by sheets of thin, surface ice of a mauve gray. Suddenly there is a thin high whistle of wings overhead and a flock of mergansers goes by in the direction of that strange arctic sun, and some heavy bodied eiders push low over the water, in a string, one following another. Over the tidal flats there are black, shiny periwinkles, now stopped by the cold, no longer roving on the sands. Aside from passing birds, this winter landscape, hushed, loaded with the cold air, moves things slowly, if they move at all. Under the weight of the sky, the landscape's forms—the engraved sands, the crystalline snowy ice, the rocks — are so definite, its law so complete unto itself, that I feel as if I could keep going down, down into it, without end.

The road is behind me, the cottages, and in a few more miles a city, then a war. I live half in confusion. The way man's world goes is unpredictable. A society changes or comes into being as part of struggle and hope, and then all of a sudden we see what its terrible limitations are, what impossible heroism is required. We devour the earth with confidence and are surprised to find that we are limiting ourselves in the process. How will we survive our genius for invention coupled with our crazy willingness to destroy? Are we casting ourselves off from all biology?

And still these continual motions of the tides, the sun and moon, this high art of a winter day, are as undiminished as that recurring desire in mankind for freedom and wholeness of action, outlasting all societies, all their tyranny of means.

For half an hour or more while the sun goes down, the observed, felt landscape is omnipotent with its ice, reflecting waters, flight of birds and responsive sky, containing all I have to meet it with and vastly more, every known language and none. Is it not enough to find electric liveness there along with an arctic sleep, to find the symmetry of distance, the motion of the globe, to hear the ice and tides, and to be able to combine in your mind the extremes of fire and frost? Is it not enough to see a slow gray gull and a brilliantly swift sea duck, and to receive night's approach after an unequalled day, to go no further than the rocks, enamelled with ice and light, and glimpse the rifts and rising in ice and in existence? It is not enough, if only because no words, no world of words, can begin to embody this surpassing unity.

VII

Cove and Forest

THE world is our polluted oyster. At the same time, we are not close to the oyster, nor do we seem capable of doing enough about the pollution. To put it in Marshall McLuhan fashion, we wear the environment like a mask. The image making and the ownership are synonymous; symbolists and materialists are one. We have built up such fantastic material systems that they stand between mankind and all his original stars. We endanger the natural environment partly because we have made so many signs for ourselves, invented the means for so many accelerated directions, cut so many corners, that we have almost forgotten how to converse with it. And our greed for applications and appliances tends to make us forget that it was the search for truth and not its substitutes that made them possible in the first place.

Technical triumph, as we find out every day, in every breath of chemically polluted air, has to conquer the logic of its own wastes. We are paying a million times more for it than we should. Half our efforts and organization goes into remedying the results of our own actions. Cleaning up gets more difficult and expensive every day. We reduce our means of subsistence, the topsoil, the plants, the animals, everything that makes for a rich organic environment, and have at the same time to produce inadequate substitutes. The tons of chemical fertilizer that make up for the lost earth go into the rivers and streams to produce excessive nitrogen. To purify the earth environment takes world effort, if the world is not too busy filling it with impurities. It is becoming too late to say that this is the penalty we pay for "progress," if only because the price is too high.

A civilization which isolates itself from its basic source of supply is weak in the limbs, and this is true not only in terms of what we call natural resources but of every living thing. What will the cities of man become when they are starved of a large part of the world's original company? The golden eagle and the polar bear are overtaken by helicopters and shot down. The lion and the antelope are dispossessed. There are only about a thousand grizzly bears left south of Alaska. The great whales have been hounded to the farthest seas. The fur seals are giving out. The wolf has been exiled. Lobsters, clams and fish are becoming scarcer. It is said that we will have to start farming the sea, which we are now filling with wastes and poisons on a major scale. We are faced with innumerable lost species and last resorts. At least mankind will have enough dead-end decisions to occupy it for a long time to come.

Perhaps we are more helpless than we know. Perhaps we are now on a convertible energy ride that will take us where it will. We may be part of a self-motivated evolution which is drifting us like plankton into the jaws of a whale. Overpopulation may also put us in the position of being so hopelessly, intensely crowded that the question of allotting room or food to anything other than human need will be academic. We will need all the room and food we can get; and any extra tolerance the earth may still allow us, because we will not have much of our own to spare.

I cannot always be sure, when I go back to a place known to me, of field or woodland, marsh or sandy shore, not only that its plants or bird life will be as I left them but that it will be there at all. I have seen too many such places disappear. I only need to stick my head out of the door to hear the roar of machines introducing oblivion to the natural world. Some other occupier stands at my shoulders wherever I go, and all of us are constantly being stuffed with excuses to ignore what we should not ignore. It seems as if, in human terms, life's particularities were free to depart.

But I believe that man in the living earth still has a choice to defend, and I think that lies between conquest and common inclusion. We have things to learn from manifested life, whether in a leaf or drop of water, such as to amaze us. In them are the secrets of form and uncommon action, as well as a sensitivity, spontaneity and cohesion which should attract us like the magnet to the pole, if we are still earthbound.

Each natural action is significant, in the place where it originates, and is in some way allied to other actions around and beyond it, and to wait on them and watch them is to learn the rightness of things. One evening I was watching a great blue heron fishing in a Maine cove. It was stalking in shallow water on the ebbing tide, with the stately patience characteristic of its race, the black and white head and spearlike yellow bill high up on an attenuated neck, the big smoky-blue wings like a frock coat. It was putting one leg forward slowly, then the other, very slowly. Patient waiting for something to come along represents an important part of a heron's existence, though it has the experience of where to go and what to expect. In any case it occurred to me that the effects of these grave and deliberate steps was to stir up fish. Each time a long-toed foot went down there was a little circle on the water where a small fish rose to the surface. Evidently the motion was such as to send them up without making them dash away. Each time they rose the heron would lean forward slightly, then jab quickly and get its food. Now this mode of action, this useful fishing technique, represents a success, an adaptation that works, and also the close fittingness of an animal and all its senses to an environment. It is the end result of a perfectibility in the universe. Going on with the usual invidious comparisons between mental man and the creatures that merely communicate by chirps and grunts (or, in the case of a Great Blue, with a loud, strangled croak), this is limited behavior. On the other hand, it is also a sensitive response, unique to the race of herons, and we feel its beauty. Taken with all the other incredibly varied modes of action, it is a harmony to be depended on.

I am not sure, to leave normal ecological grounds, that men too are not in many respects self-mesmerized, like a bird in a tree singing the same note. Though all fire in mind and complex in our attachments, ready for all kinds of artificiality until by accident we might snuff out all other lights with our own, we priests, angels and devils are still, though more mysteriously, bound in natural communication. This universal priesthood of the mind is what we are for, the grand ritual that is in itself a product of the evolutionary past. We are lazy, complaining, warring beings with fishing souls. Our catching may be part of much greater organization and deduction, but in its particularity it belongs on the same earth with the blue heron and its fish. And what is outside us, or for that matter how we can extend our inner world, is always a matter for conjecture. We do not know how much we are capable of knowing.

This saltwater cove where the Great Blue operates

may eventually be overcome by the brutal human need to domesticate nature entirely. In the meantime it is left pretty much to itself, and with a little attention to detail anyone can begin to see just how elaborate and intricate all its adjustments must be, throughout the year, by night and day, sunlight and moonlight, with the rhythms of the tide, the temperature, and many, many other factors. Every animal shows it. After the cold late winter and stormy days in early spring, barn swallows and tree swallows come in about the beginning of May to fly after the insects over the cove. These insects may be fairly high over the trees, or low over the water, depending on a daily rhythm of flights. Cold and darkness keeps them down. In the morning, attracted by the light of the sky, they may start up and be carried hundreds of feet into the air. In some cases they are "aerial parasites" whose direction is determined by the wind, and in others they may be migrants following a fairly definite course.

The swallows swerve and twist, with an almost leaf-like dipping and turning flight, as leaves are flown by the wind. They skim swiftly along the surface of the water, fly up to catch insects, then drop down again, or this cove-part of the sky is suddenly filled with them way overhead, twittering and darting skillfully everywhere.

A big white and gray herring gull lifts and glides in the currents above the trees, while gusts periodically make the water's skin shiver and move like dark clouds or sudden plume-like patterns across the cove. And underneath the water there are responses everywhere, in those animals protected by rockweed and eelgrass, in crevices between rocks and stones, in self-made holes in the wider areas of mud. This cove is continually filled and drained, being an end zone for tidewaters that rise in and lower out through its narrow rocky neck — once harnessed for a grist and saw mill — and an inlet winds behind it through banks of tidal vegetation, lost finally at the base of rocks and mounting trees. In terms of mobile animals like fish and birds and other free-swimming or water-borne forms of life, there is a change in population at each tide. The resident animals — mussels, barnacles, soft-shell clams, crabs, worms that use the basic mud bottom for their burrows — use the food that comes to them in seawater, or move out to prey and scavenge, often at night.

But even the fixed, sessile animals like barnacles have larval forms that are distributed far and wide by the sea; in their case, all over the world. The incoming waters flush and drain, bringing in marine plankton, taking detritus from one part of this cove and inlet to another, stirring up the plant life, prompting animals to move about. It is a sheltered environment, but nowhere without motion, nowhere without response of one kind or another, in the levels of the water itself, on the surface of the scattered rocks and underneath them, through the surface layers of mud.

Among the many species of animals in this area there are all kinds of adaptations, to light, to excess oxygen or the relative lack of it, to wetting and drying out, and many methods of concealment or locomotion. The cove is an inshore marine environment of course, so it is not a self-contained unit like a pond, with its own population, and in part its own climate, irrespective of what lies outside it. The cove partakes of a larger mobility; it shares a distance, with the migrant smelts that come in early spring to lay their thick clusters of eggs over the small freshwater streams that flow into it, and with the tribe of herons and ducks, with an occasional seal, and the striped bass. For all its shallow waters, it contains multiple depths.

I also feel, innate in these environmental standards, this rightness of life and place, things put down by human observation, something beyond what is visible to me. Life's undefined allowances, and not its names, are what make me stop and stare. In shallow water, back of an elbow in the cove, a group of tiny fish seem to hesitate in the sunlight, making silver flakes where they turn each other slightly aside. They tremble as they wait, sensitive to each other's actions, and to the calm water's circling and flashing in the air and light, to its self-engendered stirrings or to those they occasion themselves. They seem incomparably fragile, and true to a silence of their own, and because of them, for a little while I lose my way.

The incoming tide starts as a mere rising in water level around a periwinkle, a faint stirring in a patch of weeds, then it rushes faster through the mouth of the cove where water stress begins to show in a bucketing band of small waves. The periwinkles begin to move very slowly over the rocks. I notice a barnacle fixed to the back of one of them, and a dog whelk feeding on another barnacle, then a periwinkle riding on the shell of a dog whelk. They all move, in a sense, on various commands. They seem to be slaves of a fixed obsession in nature, namely eating. The eaters and the eaten are heaped together, or they ride each other's shells to mutual advantage. They bore in, they roll and rasp and scrape, poor creatures. But what is this immense hunger all about? Am I more or less of a creature because I live by money and yearn to make it?

The water itself, that wonderful stable medium without which we could not exist, keeps running back and forth, flowing with its special life forms, its adapted secrets. It carries the shed skins of barnacles at times, so many in any small area as to indicate an abundance beyond belief. At certain times of the year it also carries minute newly hatched fish, quivering like tiny slivers of glass; their definite black eyes contrast with their bodies' transparency, so fragile as to have a power in fragility, an artifice of growth hesitating in the balance.

A drop of this water, seen through a microscope, shows all kinds of twitching animals of the planktonic world. They are transparent, or semitransparent, long-horned, wormlike, both quick and slow. They whir and dart, or move aside slightly, these tiny, perfect fragments of life, like the hatchling fish, as if set going at some exact but delicate stage of making. Some of the single-celled plants, which can also show up in the microscope, behave both like plants and animals, as if they came out of a primitive or potential stage of life that might combine any number of attributes before dividing into one direction or another. Some of the flagellates are of this kind, able to move through the water with a whiplike motion, capturing food in the manner of animals and at the same time containing chlorophyll with which they use the surface sunlight to nourish them like plants. They are analyzable but ambiguous like the medium in which they live. When I first saw a group of these flagellates, pale green little dots, spinning through the water, spontaneously chasing from one part of it to another, I felt a wide, calm cosmos behind them, reproducing its own.

So the measure that sends things spinning on their way, from the swallows high in the air down into the water over which they fly, and carries things seen and unseen, those capable of vision or which react with relative blindness. I am only able to receive a few of the messages that pour in. But it is this almost-catching that leads me on, the teasing of a story whose very nature is to leave its outcome untold. There are samenesses everywhere of course. We spend our lives in pursuit of them. The swallow slips away and when it comes back it will not have changed its color except under the radiances of the sky. The barnacles remain with their fixed habits, for this minute or this millennium. The cove is the kind of place whose every inhabitant and element can be named, and there may be no use in challenging accuracy with nothing but my stirred and idle senses, if senses are only symbols of what they meet. But my senses give me the faith that all manifested reality is incomplete, that each thing I see owes as much to unending suspense as to any category I can find for it. The human problem is not only how to meet the challenge of truth but how to meet all life in the same world as our own, how to end the divorce between him who sets forth and him who is met, the observer and the observed. When will true communication be established between us and the objects of our eyes?

2

Self-centered beings, we civilizados tend to assume that all life proceeds on the same plane as our own, that of the horizontal, whereas in the forest most life struggles up toward the sun and at death drops away from it. It is the rhythm of living.

—Adrian Cowell, *The Heart of the Forest*

The soil is no less shifting and often precarious in its nature than the water, and when you think how thin this surface mantle is you can bless the grass and trees for holding it down. Like the tidewaters in the

cove, it is marked by sensitivities, degrees of awareness, sometimes explosive reactions, which no one
skinning off ten acres of woodland and calling it
"dirt" could possibly imagine. Just at the high tide
mark, flicking over the surface of the pools, there are
often small masses of blue-gray fleas, one of the few
marine insects, and known as *Annurida maritima*.
One day in spring there were a great many of them
showing on the slanting surface of rocks exposed between the water's surface and the belt of grass and
forest land above them. This was a zone marked by a
thin white line of salt at the top of the rock. There
were two principal masses, one where the rock slanted
in slightly, and the other below, where it shelved out,
and there was a constant exchange between them. At
their closest range, a matter of inches, the fleas were
bouncing back and forth in a frenzied way. There was
intense activity, almost a boiling made by the jumping
and twitching of these thousands of animals. Each
single one was in a state of nervous agitation, and the
nearer they came to each other the more they seemed
inspired to their crazy leaps. There was a magnetic,
raining exchange between the two groups — I find no
other way to describe it — and never before had I
been so aware of what power of affinity there is in the
communities of life. If this happens in the cool and
rocky state of Maine, how will it be in Brooklyn?

Above the tide line, above the narrow belt of
grasses and plants adapted to periodic flooding and

wetting by salt water, the forest starts. Its growth has been slashed, cut over, burned, reduced to fringes between one city and another, between one attempt on its life and the next. The part of it where I go in is more properly called a wood, since there is a field beyond it and its boundaries are constantly being chewed back by the chain saw; in fact, given a little less restraint on the part of its owners it would not take more than a few days to have it a mass of stumps and chewed-up ground. Still this area belongs with the great northern forest, and its trees insist on an appropriate longevity in spite of everything, a growth and a stature which has no obligations to any needs but its own.

We have relatively narrow means by which to approach a tree. It may be in the way, or it may have ornamental value. For those who deal in lumber it will have another; and most people do not know its name. We very rarely assume that any such silent, faithful, available plant would be able to draw any more out of us than a tacit acceptance. On the other hand, trees breathe, a slow, quiet, tireless breath, exchanging gases with the outer air. They drink, through the elaborate network of roots that thread the soil. They apparently communicate impulses from cell to cell through the thin film of cambium just under the bark. They manifest the most sensitive and elaborate connections between the earth, the air and the sunlight. They are not only a life environment for native birds and squirrels and the thousands that thread the leaf mold through their roots, as well as a passive shelter for all travelers, but their connections with animate and inanimate things might just as well be called personal. They share with the gall wasp that stings a leaf to make its gall, with the caterpillar that eats leaves or needles, and with the oriole that plucks fibers from bark for its pendulous nest.

I do not, or cannot, go very deep into what a cove or the trees above it may mean in their complexities, but the depth waits. From the centipede that makes its way through particles of soil to the tips of the highest branches the wood stretches from the roots, breathing, groaning, roaring if our ears could make its inner processes their own. Birch, oak, spruce, arborvitae, pine and hemlock, each in their way vulnerable because they have to stand and take it, unable to move like animals in search of better conditions of light, moisture and freedom from enemies, stretch next to each other, continually in exchange with their surroundings. Trees may not have "passion" attributed to them, but they endure as much competitive ardor, and disaster and tense exactitude as the rest of us. That the slaughter of forests has done great things for civilization is no reason not to respect the life of a tree.

So I walked up above an explosion of water fleas at the tide's rim into the self-made darkness of the trees, and the sensitivities, the great springs inside, remained. Modern civilization has become insulated against the trees. Occasionally, passing some northern wood where the trunks of the trees stand out in thick, solid strength, their branches rough and splintered, the undergrowth tangled and covered with briars, some residual understanding comes to me of the way the undominated land used to feel in America. I see why our greed was so much encouraged, why we are so addicted to size, and why Americans have found it more important to win than to lose. But the impetus given us by this original conflict with a wilderness appears to have lost its base. The new world is just as afflicted with raw possessiveness as the old, but it can deal with what is in its way with more dispatch, less close acquaintance.

Still and forever, a wood breathes. Also, its scene, like any other, its particular arrangements, oblige you to it in a way that is the earth's possessive way, insisting on its aptitudes, insisting on unique responses. I passed by the remnants of a woodpecker's wing, a casualty of the winter, and then the foot of a snowshoe rabbit. How does the rabbit survive the weasel, or the woodpecker the great horned owl? The trees were full of the shadows of a hazard of one kind or another, full of the meaning of endurance and escape, of vibrant existence in the measured place where it was held.

As I walked through an open space between the trees that was covered with fallen logs, vines and ferns, I flushed a white-crowned sparrow. It skipped quickly and silently ahead of me from ground level and perched in a nearby tree. Then another appeared, and both sounded their alarm calls. A little search and I found their nest, a small cup of grass next to a fallen log, surrounded by spruce seedlings and ferns. And in this green, dappled place, the nest held two eggs, of a light, flecked, tawny color like immature grapes.

There were patches of spring flowers farther on, fringed milkwort, a little pink flower with extended petals like wings, and starflowers, crisp, white and neat, and white wood anemones, each of their small flowers having the bravery of a single stem. Out of the will of beauty they lighted their own ground, each defined petal, each thin-veined perfect leaf.

A golden crowned kinglet perched nearby, its feathers blown by the wind so that they were lightly parted on its cloud-gray breast. It had a repeated tiny, low cry: "tseet, tseet," and a faint song: "tee-tee-tee-tee," with a trill at the end. Then its relative the black-capped chickadee passed through, unconcerned, as usual, by human presence. A robin whickered loudly, and an ovenbird sounded. I heard warblers with high-pitched, whispery notes, and after some searching caught sight of two of them flitting in tall spruce and white pines, one a Blackburnian, the other a black-throated green, very trim, as colorful as flowers and as exceptional. They were elusive, bright migratory notes showing that northern trees are touched by the tropics.

The wood was a matter of survival, of adaptation to the fine edges of necessity, so that the red squirrels I heard chattering in the evergreens were in the same frame as the snowshoe rabbit. Each species used it as their home range, the rabbits with trails, the squirrels with tunnels at the foot of the trees and a knowledge of them, from crown to root, which was a part of every twitch and spring they made. Hairbreadth survival depends on exceptionally clear senses finely tuned to the world they travel in.

The bright-eyed red squirrels added a magic spontaneity to the dipping arms of the trees. I remember as a boy sleeping out one night and being woken up by a red squirrel scolding from the top of a white pine for all it was worth, shaking and chattering as the dawn spread across the sky. Now on this day so many years later, I sat still under a few giant white pines, resinous of scent in the warm sun, with long, thin silvery-green needles shimmering. After a while a whole pack of red squirrels came by, chasing each other excitedly over the needles of the forest floor. One of them had a pinkish-red cast to the top of its back and tail but was otherwise white. They dashed over the needles, they ran up the trunks of the trees, skipped along the branches, ran down again and after each other, making little nasal, grunting noises as they went.

Later I moved to a spot about a hundred yards

away and met the albino again in the middle of a gay chase with two other squirrels, and since I stood very still behind a tree, one of them came right up between my feet without seeing me. It stopped spasmodically, splayed its hind legs wide, twitched and shook with alarm, then gave a little shriek and scampered off.

The trees held these spontaneous and sensitive lives the year around, or like other trees great distances away, received them when they came, being at once part of the substance of a local year and of forces thousands of miles in extent. This northern forest environment, of rabbits, squirrels, fishers and wildcats, crows, warblers in season, minks, weasels or porcupines, all using it as they could, was manifest regeneration. The young spruce seedlings were starting again, as they did around the world, crowding the slashed areas where their progenitors had come down, to battle for light and space, to take on the sun and the snow. In them was the latent power of all nature to reestablish itself. In a minute or over unseizeable periods of time, that force, sometimes totally hidden, sometimes blotted out, shows itself again, demanding its primal right again in a seed that is to fill a desert, or a needle that claims the light.

The tidewaters rose and lapped beyond the scaly trunks of the trees, whose branches lifted and fell in the rhythmic swing of the air, sounding sure and deep. An occasional strong gust would make them sound with a long "whaughh" and then would die down again, while a herring gull wheeled high and free out in the sky with a trumpeting laugh, and a green heron crouched on the rim of the tide, stealthily moving forward like a thief.

VIII

"The Lower Orders"

God keep his Oath to Sparrows —
Who of little Love — know how to starve —
—Emily Dickinson

PRESUMABLY the human race is still subject
to those physical laws whereby no organism or
group of organisms can survive beyond its capacity to
sustain a productive relationship with its environment.
This means that the earth has only so much food and
space to keep us. It also means that we need more
living sustenance than we ourselves supply. Conscious
effort may help us endure, but not without the conflicts, the foils, the attachments our experience has
always needed from the life of earth. More equations
are needed, and fewer oppositions such as superior as
against inferior beings, or man versus beast. Destroy-
ing a majority of the beasts on earth has not given us
any superiority, it may even have dangerously limited
our ability to redress the imbalance we have caused

between ourselves and the rest of life. There is nothing superior about man-made deserts of uniformity.

As I walk the crowded shore, I would prefer not to wait for our contemporary confusion of images to resolve our indecision. Let us find new images to bring us out, new symbols to declare our connections. There is nothing in the natural world which cannot be shown to hold the secrets of a dazzling elaboration, an incomparable advance, if only we will let go this idea that all traffic stops at the man-made light. The thought is more easily preached than accomplished of course, but how am I to admit the "lowly" multitudes without it? Unless I can accept some guidance from them I will not live with life.

The outer limits of human capability and possession are still what they used to be, a mystery. (I do not mean mystery as a vague substitute for understanding, but in the sense of a process with comprehensible results but incalculable scope, against which the mind might test itself forever.) Men descending eight hundred feet to the ocean bottom have to be protected in the most careful way known to us, and sending them into outer space takes the efforts of a whole civilization. The capacity of the human organism is still unknown. And the role of evolution in the emergence of the human mind is something we can speculate about indefinitely. Mystery so far as any living organism is concerned must imply that it is more than an end result, or an adapted product or a successful mechanism; it is part of the infinite sending on that produced it. Life is still precious and potentially immortal. In that sense there is no such thing as superiority, only mutual stature. If these small things provide, it is up to me to participate.

One night at the beginning of July, on a part of the North Beach, overlooking the town of Chatham, Massachusetts, I looked at the lights across the water and listened to sea airs around me over the jutting sands of a new shore. This part of the beach, an extension of a sand spit facing Monomoy Island, had been built by the sea and molded by the wind in only thirty or forty years' time. It was full of barrows and mounds. It had salt holes in it, fresh and saltwater marshes. Sharp and shiny beach grass held its sands down. Eelgrass grew in the tidewaters along the inner shore; the outer one faced the open waves of the sea. On the ground between were big bushes of Rugosa roses, with white, sweet-smelling flowers, or in various shades of red and pink. During the afternoon red-wing blackbirds had called out from the marshy areas where they were nesting — in fact they dove toward my head in great agitation when I came too close — and sparrows flocked through the thickets. There were skunk and rabbit tracks everywhere. In some areas the sand was pitted with holes made by small ants, and I could find the wolf spider's definite hole, and a sand dune locust whirred up ahead of me. This place was new, wild and clean in its placements. The air carried new scents and new sand, and it met the lipping waters along the channel's edge and rough seas on the outer shore, in a dipping and rising along the contours of the land. It swept on toward nightfall stirring sands and grasses, bringing the smell of flowers, balanced in the measures of hot sun in a hollow, and cool water under open sky. It was as if perfection, without the period of time and consolidation needed to stabilize so many natural areas, had taken over exactly and surely. This wonderful sureness whereby a spit of sand is taken care of within the evolutionary frame, made right by the life that fills all ends and corners without delay, this power of inclusion, is what no man has supplanted.

After nightfall the stars were running in wildness. They foamed overhead, with the running seas by our side. All our power of mechanical flight, our crowds, our agony, our self-abandonment or abandonment of others, our blind directness like a wheel rut in the sand, seemed nothing to this miracle. We fell in behind the flight of the universe. Yet flight was accepted there. The night, nearly passing perception, was in perception. Breath, in the closed or expanding universe, rose and fell.

I found great comfort in every living thing that used this region. It became a place of secret associations. Small lives were tunneling everywhere in the darkness. Some (the bioluminescents) made light. Some took refuge. Some devoured. Some provided. They cared for existence — only in a state of harsh necessity if you like — but under the stars I felt that light fell on their work as brightly as on their mortality or insignificance. Eluding mankind, they were still at the business of building life, and under the high, blowing darkness they told me it was equality of provision that counted most.

2

IT is hard not to view the life of earth from a disconnected point of view if we are able to kill, level out or distort almost everything we meet with relative ease — when, in point of fact, this may be public policy. Indirectly, disconnection may even be taught in the schools. The text of a science accepted as an end in itself is not necessarily carried over to life connections, either with respect to human values or the environment. Between the indoors and the sky innumerable possibilities are lost.

When you dissect a frog do you relate it to that lithe animal, the color of blond wood, spotted with black and with sides of pink, leaping away at your approach as you walk through marshy grass — in other words, the pickerel frog? Who knows much about a fish that is related to no water but that which spatters the windowpane? And perhaps even that connection is seldom made. Let us get together with the frog and the fish before we descend into abysmal ignorance. There is no reason to believe we are not allied.

How do we know that an insect's behavior is only

fixed, or patterned in automatic ways, and not motivated? The fact that a fly's brain may not weigh more than 0.84 milligram may not necessarily remove it as an animal from human analogies, careful though we have to be in making them. Watching an insect eat and fly or crawl up the wall is not only to witness a system of nerves, a unit of reflexes, but a wild thing whose behavior is part of the unified ways of earth. Why should we not explore it in terms of human intuition, our sensations and perceptions, distant though we may be? How can you not employ at least a degree of anthropomorphism in approaching the behavior of other animals? Our kingdoms are not so distinct as that.

Some analogies are farfetched, but our unwillingness to project ourselves can put a rope on all inquiry; it can also stiffen our wills to the point of disuse. To associate with what is left of the wild world is not just to farm but discover it, from the depths it touches in ourselves.

When we look at a moth or a butterfly, is fixed adaptation all we see? In other words, is this the end result of a passive interaction with the environment, mutation and heredity finally producing the moth that looks like the bark of a tree, or an insect like a flower? All these nearly exact duplications or reflections of environment should not make us forget that life itself is an actor, and not merely the acted-upon. The organic vital form plays world in its own inch, square yard, or mile of earth and water, and it too has conquered, even if it has only learned how to spin a web, or build a nest like that of a hummingbird, minute and masterful in its tight construction and camouflage. You do not have to go far to find an organic master with the stature of ages on its back.

One day toward the end of September the northwest wind was cutting across the small waves that spilled along the shore, making all kinds of crosshatchings and V marks there. Under these waves thousands of killifish were running lightly through clumps of seaweed and salt marsh grasses. They spread out and fled away fast in the sunlit waters as I waded in. Farther offshore, flocks of terns were moving on, diving into the surface as they went. It was a typically fine fall day, cool and clear, ready with all its migrations.

When I sat down on the beach again, I noticed a small spider. It was light-colored, with a black patch running diagonally over its abdomen, and a white band in the center of its body. It scurried out of the beach litter when disturbed, and when I held it in my hand it spun a silk thread out into the air. I lifted my finger, with the thread attached, and it let itself down onto the sand. When I poked it with a bit of grass it curled up and played dead. I noticed that it had a limy grayish-brown color, similar to the growth on the shells of some marine snails.

Then the little spider hurried off over the sand, or

tried to, moving frantically, its tiny legs working like mad up and down the sand grains that slipped away down their slopes as it climbed them. But finally it found the beach wrack again, the line of blackened rockweed, eelgrass and other detritus pushed in by the tides. If I had failed to keep my eye on this small animal all the time it would have vanished before me. Its color and markings worked in with the mass and individual forms of dead plant material perfectly. The white band around its middle was just the right width to make it fit in with the dried stems and bits of beach grass around it. So the spider was back and secure at last, a tight part of a beach environment and its definitions, but also, it had expressed itself before me.

3

As we diminish our environment, both physically and in terms of our attitude toward it, so we diminish our range of attention. Half the beauties of the world are no longer seen. What will we be when left to nothing but our own devices!

Where, these days, are all the monarch butterflies, folding and unfolding their handsome wings, which used to alight on flowers or cover whole trees on their fabulous migrations? How many millions have disappeared, aside from the normal cycles of population and ravages of storm and cold, because we have destroyed their environment?

Anyone who has ever seen part of the metamorphosis of the monarch must have been struck by the deep perfection of that process and its results. The caterpillar, in gray and green striped elegance, suspends, after a period of eating, on a milkweed flower, and changes into a green chrysalis. It is now a pendant made of jade, with a ring of bright gold and tiny dots at the base. After some days the chrysalis darkens and then there is the emergence, the final change, and the orange and black beauty hangs with its fresh and beautifully patterned wings folded, pumping blood into them slowly. I remember such a one, newly sprung into the world. Disturbed, it had unfolded its wings and flown off for a short distance. The season was autumn, with the leaves half off the trees, and it was in the evening toward sundown. The insect landed on a shadbush whose sparse leaves, orange and yellow, hung down against a dark gray trunk and a darkening, streaked sky. Joining the leaves, it hung with fresh, folded wings. There it was, for a short life and a long migration, declaring longevity to have no greater import than the time it takes me to spit in space. The monarch's existence was as sure as any other, ready in the air and light, knowing the sky and the flower, evening or dawn, cold and heat. Turning to it, or any other living thing in readiness, I might find the right key to another of the earth's infinite supply of locks.

You never know what you will see, turning over another stone, taking time out to watch what for your looking would not seem of much importance. There is a willingness which adults have to cultivate and keep alive, which childhood, in a less practiced world, never needed. I saw a small boy take his first look at a box turtle not long ago. He had no name for it, no classification, no facts and no place. He simply saw it, in its shape, its acceptable, unfrightening strangeness. When it lifted its flat head and red eyes and started to go, he said: "It's moving!" The very young meet rarity without fuss or consternation. New life comes in out of nowhere, no matter how many filing cabinets we own.

I suppose there is no use belaboring the trials taken, the endurance needed past childhood, but perhaps even they have something to say about unfinished ways, the perception erased by laws of attrition and experience, the newness gone because we have been deprived of it in ourselves, the price of exposure. And still, ignoring age, the novelty of being and consciousness — their terror too — beats at the barriers. We become aware by self-use of the incompleted nature of all things.

4

EACH of the small lives in the lower kingdoms occupies a drop of water, a blade of grass, an inch of bark or a foot of soil. There is no part of the globe that is not their habitation. And in any discoverable sense, *what* they are, though this is almost inseparably bound with *where* they are, is just as arresting as the ecological niche they belong to.

There is a field I know above the sea which is a sea of its own. On a warm September day the grass, thick from not having been cut this year, with long dried out pale stalks, sways in the wind. There is a sky shine on the field. Clumps of goldenrod shake in the running airs as they hold their pollen-laden fingers to the sun, and the asters, or "frost flowers," some white and others in shades of lavender and pinkish purple, have petals that seem to wheel in the bright air and almost ask for attention. Along the borders of this field the wind sounds through the trees like surf. Yellow butterflies dance slowly over the tops of the grasses, and a red admiral, and a monarch. A big green dragonfly, that water-born predator with compound eyes, goes whizzing back and forth, then catches an insect and lowers down on the grass to eat it. The swales of grass are cut through here and there with paths made by deer.

I look down at the flower of the white aster, and there, almost invisible in the brownish part of a blossom going to seed, is a light-brown spider. It moves only slightly when I touch the plant, but quickly, and with what seems to me a hint of ferocity. Brushing through the grass sends up clouds of tiny insects, and makes the grasshoppers jump like bits of twigs or pebbles flicked away between your thumbnail and your forefinger. There are little black crickets as well, with antennae constantly stopping, flicking around, playing out in front of them. Pale thin moths fly up and then alight on the grasses again, concealed in them by their own autumnal shade. Bees — honeybees and bumblebees — hum and swing above the goldenrod. A wasp hovers low over the ground. I caught sight of a stinkbug with its extraordinary shield of a head, and a lace wing, pale green with delicate, diaphanous wings. With what extravagance the so-called mindless are imbued!

Out of the field comes a shrilling and clicking, a steady chorus rising up into the air, the mutual response of many crowds to a season, an acclamation of a kind, created from a term of need. The air is right, the light warm, the day fine for all walkers, wanderers, darters and hoverers, intensely active, full of color and various motion, this side of the winter death to come.

Let me not impute too much of my human nature to them, or too little of their own. I passed through their strange country. I only brushed by their special corners of reality. We reacted from a distance, but in the same field.

IX

Meetings in the Field of Life

Now I know that revelation is from the self, but from *that age-long memoried self* that shapes the elaborate shell of the mollusc, and the child in the womb, that teaches the birds to make their nests; and that genius is a crisis that joins the buried self for certain moments to our trivial daily mind.

—William Butler Yeats

THE field of life, and not the landscape, garden, or even wilderness, terms we use to define our relationship with nature, this cosmic field, is where the hunting is. How could an Indian or an Eskimo, following his prey without help from guns and machines, risking his life each time he went out to hunt, not know himself to belong to the same earth as his quarry? How, since he was so near in self and in spirit, could he not venerate the powers that give and take away, and even ask forgiveness of that animal he was about to kill?

Now, since the distance has lengthened so greatly between us and direct earth sustenance, that kind of hunter is rare. We have flung ourselves out into the open by merely following the logic of cultural advance and importunity, helped vastly by war, so that each experiment in some dominating tool gives impetus to another. There is a new hell of homelessness, in a great new world covered with man-made deserts and artificial barriers. We have created a Dante-esque hierarchy, not of sinners (if sin is not to be recognized as such), but of belligerents and complainers lost in the pursuit of time. So we are divided, all together, in a wilderness of our own making. We see a nature of our own, full of harsh, searing, sudden discoveries, and meet the old one, of which our physical-chemical selves are still a part, as if it were something to be tinkered with, mastered or brushed aside. We have not the least idea whether our meddling in heredity or the creation of life substance will have responsible results or not. Perhaps, if it takes ruin to right us, we are closer than ever to first principles. The universe of loss and gain, furtherness and nothingness, will never be circumvented by human power.

At the same time, I feel there is still an attachment in me, as a representative human being, which has never been fully allowed, a giving and a going over to the rest of life which I will never manage, but which is worth trying. I live in a world of ultimate risk, cut off from almost all but human problems, while the deer and the squirrel adapt as best they can. Perhaps they know who and what is in the ascendancy these days and bide their time until something else tries its hand at running the world. But I know that the field of life is still out there, not only ready to endure the analyzer, but also in wait for the hunter, or lover in us, as if no one had ever come before. It is a vast area of unguessed beauty and sensitivity. How can we be sure we will not find ourselves there again?

I wonder, when men talk about their lonely fate on the friendless shores of the universe, faced by a savage nature which they can only deal with by taming, whether they are not really extolling their helpless pride? When a whole civilization is bent on eliminating "the undesirable effects of the external environment," including bites, storms, animals which compete with man for food and space, "trash fish," "weeds," vines that trip you up, and old age, it is applying wholesale methods and should expect wholesale results. What we eliminate is everything in the life of earth that saves us from choking to death on our own diet. We need the kind of dialogue with earth which does not always put us in the position of standing over the cash register telling everything else how much it is worth. We need to have the question asked of *us*. Much of nature cannot talk back in our terms. It needs our approach, hat in hand. We have to meet death-in-life, whether we like it or not. If we are not afraid of that (or perhaps it is better to say, if we recognize our fear), then we will not meet life as strangers.

I go down to look at the ocean again for the five

hundredth time. There it is, in calm blue plains, or heaving and rough, ending in seething beds of foam along the beach, always holding that pivotal sweep with respect to the land and the horizon. And it takes me for nothing — a just and honest fate for all beginners. Here is the ambiguous face of nature or general existence, and I look for attachments across its surface, the bird, or classic wave. One day in October as I stood on the cliff's edge above Cape Cod's Outer Beach at Nauset, I remembered facing a spruce tree on the Maine coast at about the same time the year before. The tree's bark, with small, scaly plates, was black in the rain and spotted all over with gray-green lichen. The rain was coming down heavy, hard and straight in the darkening evening. I was confronting a tree and also the sea beyond it, and I felt some deep outer relationship I was unable to name, something that could not be described as "enigmatic," "unfeeling" or "inanimate." I do not want to be any more obscure and pantheistic about it than I need to, but there was a calm, savage, assured silence there, of a kind that was as distant from me — to be guessed at — as the first star about to shine above the spires of the forest. The wild night noises of the wind came through later on. The land itself seemed to go on saying that even if all its trees were cut down its very bareness could only prove its inviolate, untouchable nature, its existence as a power in the universe, cold and grand as the sea.

On that October day the following year I looked

down over the rim of the sea's broad table. I heard the grinding moan of the surf, and saw a black cloud of ducks far out, coming in sight from fairly high in the air. Then they moved closer to the surface, spread and thinned out, hovered, rearranged themselves in flight and settled down on the sea. They joined hundreds of dark scoters already there at the line of breakers beyond the beach. These birds rode imperturbably on top of the big incoming waves, letting themselves float up and down their troughs and walls, and just as a wave broke over them, or a second before, they dove down below the surface to come up again after it had passed. On the other hand the gulls that were scattered there too, being not so skilled in riding the waves, would fly up before they broke.

Occasionally there would be an exchange of a few ducks between the various flocks. I watched one fly low over the water, with a scoter's hurried and at the same time sturdy flight, then brake itself a little over one group of its fellow ducks, lowering down as if to land. But it kept going, passed over another group, circled around a third, then came hurtling back to land among the first it had hesitated over. So an organization had been confirmed, a decision made. Probably it had to do with whatever age or sex group the bird could best keep company.

As the scoters rode the breakers to the manner born, gulls flew by with their measured wingbeat or stood along the beach lined up in small groups, five to twenty feet apart, occasionally shifting their position by stiff little walks along the sand. I admired the calm ease of a black-backed gull as it cruised by, banking in the air above the surfline. I walked the cliff edge and when I peered over it the gulls nearest to me flew up and away, traveling off easily: "My masters in flight," I thought, "and brothers in opportunism." One of the black, heavy-bodied scoters had been sunning itself on the beach, and I watched its ungainly, ducklike stance as it waddled back into the water. Each to it medium, in the great undulating plains around us, with a new assignment in balance from life to life, generation to generation, the birds flying up or ducking easily and the waves like compared ideas and definitions, running on into the future.

Then where I stood at the land's drop-off, above the whole Atlantic, I turned back, and saw a pair of pigeon hawks, dark brown in color, flying in mutual ease, rising and dipping where the contours of the cliff top rose and dipped. In their aerial skill, the display of paired keen flight, swallowlike, in their sinew and blood, for the shape and shaping of the air, in their being wedded, each to the other, bound in grace and facility, was the earth's surprise, its gift, its unsurpassed, most loved success.

2

THERE is no such thing as mechanical evolution, except as limited human hands apply it. The end product is endlessness. Every act and its revelation, a hole in the sand, the shaking of the grass, the scoter's easy riding, is composed of measure and the unmeasured alike. The hawk belongs to the earth's continuous making, and if I belong there too I see the hawk as one to another, I and you. It is not so much that everything has to be found out as that it still has to be met with. Along this same shore I have never had to assume a great deal. I have been given as much as I have found.

Sometimes the fog closes in, and the air, the sky, the sides of the sea come closer, as well as the associations I take with me. I come on a crow pecking in the litter at the head of the beach and it flies up at once on big black wings and becomes a kind of nervous neighbor with crackbrained thoughts. The human race is a queer lot and there is no telling where their violent imagination or quirks will take them next. And there is starvation in Africa, despair in India, division and anxiety in America, compulsive inhumanity in every land. I do not know where to turn. Deep in fog, with the clatter of pebbles and the heavy sound of the surf, I am forced to think about endurance and whether it will sustain me, and conflict, not to be solved within the hour. Narrow corners and sudden walls, hard meetings and secret lives are mine.

But alongside my thoughts, my fitful advances, goes the enormous ease of all the waves. Then the sand sings a little under my feet, and I hear a muttering of gulls at intervals, and then the low honking of geese through the fog. I am aware of a global wheeling that never stops, taking the size of agony, the stature of trial with it. There is a corresponding spin in us which needs to be set going for survival's sake. I feel the earth's great vigor of deployment. The birds travel hard and out of sight. Fish circle and pulse under seawater. The earth, to include us, must have a passionate heart. I begin to hear its various singing, the profound forms moving through water and air, the sounds of a major unity.

Once, on such a walk down the beach, as I was trying to dispose of my confused thoughts, or perhaps develop some useful new ones, I saw the omnipresent tribe of gulls offshore. They were mewing and crying. Some were skirmishing over the food they were after in the shallow waters, chasing each other up and down, back and forth. Or they stood by themselves with a do-nothing air, then lifted up after a while into the wind and flew over side-swinging water lanes across the flats. Their choked calling sounded all the time, in the repetitive exercise, assured, even smug, of their society and its business. And suddenly I had a feeling of relief and elation, and I yelled out some greeting to them, as though all I needed was this encounter.

To hail a herring gull, say hello to a clam, or take some vocal joy from the flight of a hawk, may seem eccentric. I have, on several occasions, spent time in the close company of an injured gull or crow, and once a brown thrasher. They kept their own counsel, to say the least, so much so, I think, that no patterns I had ever learned about from the writings of the behaviorists seemed to fit them. They had their cut of the cosmos, and I had mine. They had the refuge of their own jitters or the inability to communicate. But it is not that I have anything to say that would be useful to other animals, or even plants — after all I have a hard enough time in human society in that respect. It is only that I like to feel free to express our mutual company with or without returns. More than that, if the world of nature and the world of man are to be involved in a continued partnership — and this would seem essential to our vitality — then we share a great dimension, where none of us, in what we say or how we say it, or how we keep silence, are without importance. I greet the gulls so as to avoid making too many exceptions between my neighbors.

Men are committed not only to the transcendent power of the mind but to the seizures of life. Nor is it simply that love and our despair in losing it makes the human world go round — the main thing is that we are involved with one another to the bitter end, not only in a struggle for existence but a struggle with it. And still I do not know what better depth to call upon in meeting the life of earth. What we experience is part of the reconciliation of opposites, heat and cold, night and day. Human conflict is another aspect of the possibilities of energy, the relentless trying out of universal matter in motion. The part which is played by human choice may seem ever more strange and mysterious, but in terms of human turmoil and behavior we are no farther removed from this fiery, breathing earth, shrugging with earthquakes as it goes, than were our remote ancestors.

Furthermore, no biological advance keeping human beings almost indefinitely alive — though in what state? — overrules the principle that the basic, acceptable risk for man, or gull, or snail, having been given life, is to lose it. Nor do I think that if man can create life out of chemical synthesis he is necessarily a great deal farther ahead than he used to be. How do you define the responsibility of creation, and its limits? Is that what we are in fact doing? Does it not imply a re-creating, a sending ahead interminably? We do not have unlimited genius. And it would be hideous to join in creation, to intervene in evolution, and not be able to bear the responsibility for what we had created. Why this scarring business of playing God? Is this not our last chance to play at being man?

To make everything our own is to make too little of too much. Greed is not a special commodity but universal. Even, or especially, little boys know that taking needs sharing to keep its balance. I met two of them on the beach, one four years old and the other six, so they told me. I showed them the egg case of a skate, and then I told them how a clam worm eats. Worms excite disgust: "Agh!" Then we found the globular shell of a moon snail, and then, when I asked how barnacles eat, the oldest boy said: "Oh, I know about them already."

Then they said: "Let's find some more." So we collected, not for any other purpose than to have the thing, to pocket it, to know its reality, and the boys insisted on the rights of sharing: "I gave you one of mine. You give me yours." And we mutually accept that, and we share.

I left them behind me, to meet the inevitable gulls again, to hear the magisterial croak of a black-back and watch a herring gull soar easily overhead. Two black-bellied plovers ran as though in tandem across the tidal shallows, a shadow for each. Then a flock of semi-palmated plovers flew, or swung in, close to shore, making a sharp whistle with their wings that had the quality of squeaking wood. With a last fling into the air, a flip and a dash, they settled down on a rim of sand — a flight of neatness, abandon and dexterity all in one. Along the banks of an outgoing creek farther on there were a few other birds, their heads tucked in, resting, while wave impulses licked along the edge of the bank like musical notes. Sanderlings hurried forward at the line where beach and water met, almost shaking from side to side as they went. There was something about their twinkling forward and stopping to feed, their going on again, loosely and at the same time interconnected, that made me think of little fears running together for company. They

acted almost as if worry were a part of their characteristics as a race. (I suddenly hear a voice saying: "Can
sanderlings make gravity bombs?" That, as I understand it, is the latest projected advance in complete
annihilation, and of course nothing on earth could produce one. We are special and even, if you like, un-
natural in that — or almost with a Nature of our
own. Yet what does such a weapon come down to but
ultimate worry?)

One sanderling pecked quickly over the rockweed
covering a big boulder offshore which was being
rhythmically passed or hit by the waves. Just as a direct wave was about to break, the bird would casually
flit into the air as if without looking, and then return.
Farther along, a three-year-old herring gull was pecking away at a small flounder on a sandbar, pecking at
it, lifting and dropping it again. A second flew in and
landed near the first, which uttered a long call, while
the newcomer stood rigidly by. Both called together,
and the second, having obeyed the ceremony of threat
and response to threat, flew off. The original owner then
banged away at the flounder some more, to be interrupted shortly by a big black-back and another herring gull which now caused it to fly up, and, after a
chase, drop its fish. Herring gull number three then
picked up the fish and managed to swallow it whole
where it stood on the sand, seeing to it that the drama
had the right ending from its point of view.

From point to point under these soft skies and the

rhythmic association of waves and distance, boys, birds and men shared the world. Order, placement and control, with a basic grasping from far and wide, came to this shore, and that we should meet one another in this context, that we encountered common response, belonged to no race in particular — which was all, for the time being, I needed to know.

X

The Sea of Survival

THE DEPTH

Blood hears
a thing of the heart,
booming at sundown,
where flowers,
light's showers,
thresh the waves
the skies ask for.
Down again, fish.
Sound out that faith
which feels
flame for the drowned,
sea wounds,
bound bells,
currents in dawn —
the cruel roaming
of no thing
but salt and sorrow
bring or borrow,
ebb and boom,
the sea steers
wind rises for.

THE shore calls from season to season, place to place. One autumn day in Maine, there was a sea flying light between the islands. The wind crashed through the spruce trees and a long swell rolled in with the incoming tide and the cold waters sloshed in the coves. Violet asters and goldenrod bloomed in the clear light, in this cool, hanging season with its special shine. Guttural but lilting gull music sounded over the glittering tides. All the islands with their pinionlike spruce pointing into egg-blue skies or seeping sunsets seemed forever moving. And out in this rock-based but water-won world, I began to feel a release into an order of timelessness.

I had been walking with my son, then five years old, and after a while he mentioned a house we had only just seen, in the way that children do before they have been trapped by the problems of time. "Remember?" he asked, as though it had not been fifteen minutes but months or years ago. "Remember how it was?" And I realized just how caught up with present anxieties I was — poor preparation for a season that called me out so beautifully. How can a man like myself, soaked with news, his senses muffled, shielded by the mechanics of his civilization and worn into despair by its brutalities, how can he know the real earth when he meets it? How can he be fit company for it? Common ground waits over the water. The signals of distance shine out, and again I fail to respond.

A few hundred yards offshore was a small rocky island where herring gulls and a few eiders bred every year. We took a dory and rowed out. I had been there in the spring when the gulls had kept flying around in a high crying cloud waiting for me to leave. I had seen their downy chicks, of a dusty speckled color that shaded into the rock itself. They hid in crevices or they crouched down on the bare rock or in scanty nests made out of dried grasses and stringy rockweed. Now there were no gulls, though there was a rank smell of guano on the island as we walked over it. Bits of crab shell were scattered around and there were little heaps of clam and mussell shells, and a number of gull bones. By the size of the bones, I guessed that there must have been considerable mortality among young gulls almost old enough to fly. Perhaps some had died of food poisoning. Mortality hung in the air in any case, and its evidence covered the raw rock. This was a place where life was started and defended by bold, zealous parents. This was also where risk, death and danger were joined at a casual level, primitively accepted. Herring gull chicks, like the young of all birds, are highly vulnerable and may die of exposure if left accidentally by their parents for too long, or killed by a marauding black-back or even an adult of their own species if they stray too far from their nests. But in the interests of survival an order is sternly maintained, a depth of protectiveness acted upon. Many more gulls are brought into the world and inherit the earth's great standards which require that every life be ready to balance the burning of all others. There are no compromises on this level of existence; and that might make a man shiver a little on a cold autumn day, but exposure is what we need.

It may be hard for a civilization built on waste to understand that, in spite of a vast mortality and a using up in nature, nothing is thrown away. The expenditure is not unilateral but for the sake of all things. Nothing is without its value, therefore nothing is waste. What appears to be merciless or cruel to us is merely a factor in munificence. This is like the sea, which may seem heartless to those who have to live with it directly. At the same time, men have always accepted it and even had a lifelong need for it. One slip into that cold, mountainous surf lunging against the rocks along the outer shores of Maine and Canada, and I might well be done for. I come back to stare and stare again at that vast roaming and resounding, full of a fire of associated lives, and it gives me back nothing but an anonymity; but I require it.

That one sea is both a builder and a destroyer. I look at the barnacles along the shore and wonder what can be said about these bleak, restricted lives, so lost in numbers. Along thousands of miles of rocky shores covered and uncovered by the tides there are often thousands of them covering one square yard. But it occurred to me one day as I saw barnacles in broad white bands and masses spread across the rocks that they were not only arrested, fixed creatures of their appropriate zones between the tides, but that they were an expression like the waves, spilled and breaking along the shore. They were living marks of the sea.

Within their vast populations the barnacles fight for living space, having to grow larger and build higher stalks to get above their neighbors. They smother and crowd each other out, and their mortality is so fantastic that the term becomes almost meaningless. In early spring, colonies of tiny ones cover bare rock with white rosettes. They are almost too small for the eye to see the line where the paired top valves meet on their shells. In six weeks they have grown twice as big. The race is on. Each shrimplike animal that lives inside one of these calcareous castles is hermaphroditic, but though it contains both sexes, it fertilizes its neighbors by thrusting a sperm tube into the valve openings of the shell closest to it. Eggs develop inside the parent barnacle and are hatched out into free-swimming larvae, which become part of the marine plankton for a few weeks of their lives. They then attach themselves to a rock or other surface, after, apparently, exploring an area for appropriate chemical stimulae. Each larva proceeds to settle down to build a shell, in which it may live for months, or under optimum conditions, with enough room to itself, for four or five years. In the process it loses its sight, and takes up adulthood in a self-made reproducing and feeding chamber. It spends its time opening and shutting its valves, depending on the rhythm of the tides, as it feeds on the microscopic food in seawater. The barnacle brings this food in to its body by means of feathery appendages that sweep out and back every few seconds. Barnacles go through the fundamental hazards of crowding, over-population and competition, of being eaten too, by dog whelks, certain kinds of fish and starfish. They use the basic food of the sea, without having to chase after it. They reproduce indefatigably. When they are actively feeding, their movements have a light and rhythmic grace like everything else which is attuned to basic energy. They have rudimentary senses, especially during their larval period. Otherwise there may be no point in trying to extend their primal attributes beyond the sea that washes over them and the rocks they populate. But though they are made of darkness and perishability, they are also marvels of survival. That they live on such spare and fitting terms with their great marine environment is something men can give them credit for.

2

BECAUSE of the accelerated speed now characterizing human culture we look at the primitive grandeur of sea or mountain somewhat obliquely. We are afflicted with univeral mobility. We are also in danger of becoming too crowded for those links with universal life which are forged by solitary and private attention. The result of this offsetting, so as to make the natural world a thing apart from human impetus, is also to make it a new and perhaps more unacceptable unknown. Since we know less about it, we may like it less. Since we find in ourselves all kinds of alienated feelings and barely controlled aggressiveness, we look to our original animal nature for a base and a solution, but our culture seems to have buried it too deep to find. Though we may be as mild and tame as sheep and capable of standing in line all day long, our scientific-technological world keeps us on the run, uncertain of its outcome. Also, we may cause violence and turmoil simply because we are obsessed with the idea that it is going to happen. We are dangerously free to travel on our own, and to make all things possible.

How hard it is, in such an age, to realize that the sea of life, the wilderness around us, is intrinsically, overwhelmingly calm! Perhaps that calmness shocks us, the way people are shocked by the will to live of a sandshark — its staying power is as disturbing as its voracity. The unvisited sea keeps its savage and capacious counsel. It makes the fish fry leap and skip in a silver rain across the surface, escaping their enemies. It makes the barnacles wave their feathery feet, and the snails crawl and the silver herring school. Its great shifting currents, dark depths and light surfaces, its varying bottoms, from shelves to ravines, its reconciliation and embodiment of temperatures, its running range, give quickness to some, slow deliberate motion to others.

At the same time, marine communities are not immune from permanent damage at human hands. We wholesalers can overfish the sea, dump radioactive wastes into it, pollute its shores with oil, and we will have proved again, as we have on land, that we have no power in and of ourselves to recover what we have destroyed. The lonely steppes of the seas will still roll and shine beyond our loss, a loss it seems to me, not only of natural resources, but of a basis for stability.

Most of these communities, except to those who are able to descend into the depths and look around them, are invisible as we stand on the shore, but there is plenty of local evidence of just how rich and intricate they can be. The tide pools along rocky shores are wild gardens, peopled with animal life. Their purity is constantly made possible by an exchange of tidal waters, though others beyond the reach of normal high tide are only filled with water by storm waves or rain. Even these high-level tide pools have a scanty population of algae, snails or barnacles. Rocky slopes, from the highest touch of salt water to the depths beyond the low tide mark, are covered with plant and animal life which hint at an almost miraculous affinity, a closeness and balance of organism and ground, foot by foot and yard by yard.

The starry foam of the surf rushes in through rock channels all gleaming on their sides with dark rockweed. In the low tide areas slick, shining belts or ribbons of kelp, cleanly clipped, wave and swing in the water. Low, thick, curly fronded tufts of Irish moss cover the rocks and the sides of pools farther up, a dark purple in warm seasons, and sometimes brownish yellow when bleached by the sun, and in the winter a reddish-brown. The tide pools extending down the rock, tier on tier, level after level, have various kinds of amphipods in them, darting through the water as thick as fleas. Green sea urchins cluster along the walls on lower levels; when the sunlight is on them their spines are alive with yellow-green luminosity, a living response in color. Some of the rock surfaces are patched with rose algae, or tufted with coralline algae, which has frosty-colored tips on crisp fronds of purplish pink. Brick red or pink starfish are collected here and there. There are sea slugs, cream-colored and covered with plumelike creations, or milky white and red, sliding slowly over the seaweed. Orange-brown horse mussels lie in the clear water at the corners and bottoms of the pools, with their shell lips partly opened, as well as the blue mussels with their blue-black to violet shells. At Pemmaquid Point, Maine, a long stretch of the lower shore has been moulded by the sea so as to make a carved series of tide pools, basins with rock partitions having rounded rims, interconnected in some areas like a maze. Their low walls, dark and slippery, also reminded me of the ribs of wrecked ships stranded on the shore. The sea has settled these pools with all the organisms I have named and many more.

The Pemmaquid region consists of a massive, bare outcropping plunging into the sea, a force standing in with force. Great broken-off slabs and columnlike pieces of schist lie around on the surface. The surf wells up against the rock and the waves' wreathed tonnage breaks, sending spray over its resistant heights. There is a monumental confrontation in the place, miles deep of geologic pressure, faulting and tilting, millennia of weathering, the rising and falling of the seas. Everything is out and open under a sky that contributes its own monumentality.

The surf rushes in to a cove below this rocky height to jostle its round boulders and make its stones clatter up and down a series of wide, water-smoothed runnels like so many bowling balls. The boulders are as smooth as pebbles and come in ovoid shapes and in all sizes, or they look like French bread when encrusted with algae, gleaming brownish-red in the sunlight. It is a wonderfully inviting little cove, full of roar and rattle, full of shape and gleam, and with the kind of assortment and variety of material that could make shopkeepers and aestheticians happy forever. I turned over a stone on one of my visits there to find a marine existence I had never been aware of before. It was dark brown, moist and limp, a little like a tadpole, and it curled up when I disturbed it, which may have given it a better purchase on the rock. It turned out to be a "sea snail," a fish equipped with a sucking disk under the forepart of its body which it uses to hang on to rocks or seaweed. Its skin was without scales, though it had fins and a tail like a fish. In any case, the

sea snail seemed a remarkable kind of hybrid animal,
and also gave me another insight into marine tenacity
and what are to me its still unimagined forms and
relationships.

The sea snail, the plumèd slug, the mussel, and a
great number of other marine organisms, live in a
world which is undeniably limited with respect to their
range or choice of action, and their senses are on the
whole primitive. Light-sensitive cells in the skin of a
marine worm are hardly comparable to the human
eye. The mysterious human brain is millions of years
ahead of the collection of nerve aggregates in a sea
anenome. But a tide pool in which we find these animals, sharing color and beauty in our perception of
them, is one of the first of worlds, where life began. I
look down through the water into primal capacity,
and all its creatures, crawling, scuttling, swimming,
moving very slowly, staying still, are joined in a community of response. Survival means sensitivity.

A tide pool is a world of vibration, light and
shadow, of slight currents, sudden inrushing waves,
and the withdrawal of waves, of changes in temperature and in the nature of the water, and its lives meet
all these influences directly. The worm or clam closes
up or pulls into a hole when a shadow falls over it.
Small fish dash into a corner in response to a vibration. The jaws and spines of a sea urchin react spontaneously to touch. Many of these animals are ap-

parently able to orient themselves by eye spots that tell them from which direction the sun is coming, others are equipped with organs that enable them to keep their equilibrium in the water, informing them of the direction of the force of gravity. All, no matter how limited their senses, react to some form of stimulus in the environment.

A tide pool is a kind of outer world to most of us, full of elemental reaction. It is just as central to this planet as any habitat claimed by man, and, in a primitive sense, some of its inhabitants may know more than we. Consider the limpet that grazes over an area of rock and then returns to the exact spot it came from. How do we explain this powerful centrality in so simple a life?

To look at some of the sea's lives is to come face to face with unknown degrees of receptive feeling. I look at a lobster in an aquarium and it is certainly a foreigner to me, though with suggestions of intelligence and even of possible mischief in its behavior. It moves through the water with a high, somewhat hobbling gait, but with its stalked legs and pincered feet working all the time. Its antennae wave limberly out in front of it. It can swim upright when it needs to. It can shoot backwards with sudden speed. A lobster's eyes are evidently not very keen; it locates objects and finds its way by feeling and smelling, since its body is covered with many tactile and olfactory hairs, or setae. A lobster can store its food, move stones aside, tear up your aquarium and make you bleed if it catches you, inspiring you to conversation or a curse; but what seems most clear, aside from the fact that it may have something like an individual personality, is that here is a creature whose senses are acutely attuned to its medium. I look at this plated animal and marvel at such closeness to a world of water, the ability to feel the slightest vibrations, ripples and currents, and to detect whatever scents may come to it as it prowls over the ocean bottom.

There is a great space between us and the inhabitants of the sea, in spite of our rational knowledge of evolutionary kinship, but in that may lie respect. Many students have enlarged their horizons with a slug. Our need for an open, functioning world environment must take all its lives into account, all that have succeeded, during the course of evolution, in surviving, as part of a tide pool, along a sandy beach, or a thousand miles of coastal seas. To have survived is an honor for any species in earth history, and we have many from which to learn. We might further learn, by right of a line that goes from fish to man, more about the power and particularities and balances of the sea, and its multitude of allied senses.

To meet the sea may be more direct and personal than we landed vertebrates suspect. Many a man has begun to learn who he was by being a follower of something no more or less significant than a fish.

Many a wandering observer like myself, when the sunset at Pemmaquid turned the great sea-wet rocks along the shore into smoking barrows and fire pits, and the small things went into darkness, felt that his inner cognizance had far to go, that all he knew was an alliance without specification except as it was written on rocks and sky. All he knew was that what he had survived so far was life, and that what he would not survive was life; but also, something in him, though he was alone like other men with little light, felt the hint of an incalculable creativeness at the massive depths of things, which might be a madness to touch upon.

It may be true that men and nature will never arrive at an appropriate relationship; at least not through conscious effort entirely, but rather through a setting to rights on the part of universal energy, which might imply that we had brought the world to a disastrous state. That would be inevitable if we were anachronisms, on a raft in space, with the rest of nature considered to be our unfeeling, brutal and often inefficient counterpart. It is a point of view which gives us the right to be as distant and destructive as we want. In reality, we can now put our ax to any tree. But the available world, the whole earth with its sea of life, still has its correspondence to a home, somewhere inside us. We have a choice, to keep that home as our starting point, or throw it away. In the long run we have to exercise our will to belong as much as to move things to our purpose. We are still in the hands of a universality which is completely indifferent to any methods taken to circumscribe it.

XI

The Dovekie and the Ocean Sunfish

IT was in December and a slight snow had started. Inland of Cape Cod waters there was very little wind, and the flakes were spaced far apart. They seemed to hover. They would lift and dip, then slant down and touch slowly to the ground. The day was gray and quiet, tempered by the even recital of falling flakes, with a dull sky and a strip of gray sea in the distance. I watched the snow flakes acting in the space around me, over and inside and by each other in slow periods, and then I drove down to the Outer Beach.

The surf there was roaring, and hard wet flakes of snow came in heavily, driven by a seaward wind, and made my eyes smart. The curled-over, breaking waves were glassy green in the gray day and pushed in soapy sheets of foam along the sands. The ocean itself seemed full of kingly mountains meeting or withholding, conflicting, pushing each other aside, part of a collective immensity that could express itself in the last little bursting spit of a salt bubble flung out of the foam that seethed into the beach, a kind of statement of articulated aim out of a great language still untamed.

Out on those cold looming and receding waters seabirds rode. There were flocks of dark brown and black-and-white eiders a few hundred yards beyond the shoreline. Gulls beat steadily along the troughs of the waves. Then I caught sight of thirty or forty dovekies, the chunky black and white "little auks" that come down from the far north during the winter to feed off the coast. Their color showed clearly against the green water, white under black heads, black backs and wings, with little upturned tail feathers. They dipped continually into the water, so quickly as to escape my notice much of the time. They made fish flips into those tumultuous sea surfaces as easily as minnows in a gentle pond.

The dovekie (called little auk in Europe) breeds by the millions in the high Arctic, principally in North Greenland, Spitzbergen, northern Novaya Zemlya, and Franz Joseph Land, with scattered colonies in subarctic areas. Drift ice is their principal habitat. They like areas where the ice is not too densely packed, and they feed in openings or leads between the ice floes, on small crustaceans in the plankton. They seem to avoid the warm waters of the Gulf Stream, following the Arctic currents instead. Especially during periods of great population growth, emigration flights of the dovekies take them on long journeys which scatter them to many regions, and occasionally take them inland in dovekie "wrecks" where they may be killed or injured, and become vulnerable to many kinds of predators. Their short narrow wings make it difficult, though not impossible, for them to take off from inland areas. One winter I saw many dead ones scattered down the Cape Cod highway, little "penguin-like" birds unknown to most car drivers.

These dovekies off Cape Cod waters were flying and diving, casting their bodies back and forth between air and water like so many balls. Their speed is not great, but when they fly off over the water their wingbeat is very quick, and their landing and diving is done with a dash and play that belies their stumpy appearance. In fact a dovekie in flight, though it lacks the agility and swinging maneuverability of a swallow, is at the same time somewhat reminiscent of those birds, with its short wings alternately beating fast and gliding, like a swift. When they swam under water these chunky little "pineknots" did so with a quick, supple, almost fishlike beat, making me think that fins after all were not so far removed from wings.

Not visible, though they brought it with them in some measure these vast distances down to New England, was the grandeur of the Arctic, whose auroras, growling ice and sunsets I could only imagine. Dovekies breed in bare heaps of rock that cover great screes, hillsides of stone, sloping down to the sea. They arrive in there in the spring when green begins to show through frozen ground and rivulets and water-falls begin to sound while the dovekies themselves utter a watery, twittering, trilling call. There they dot the slopes in great numbers "like pepper and salt," it says in *The Birds of Greenland*, and fly about "in huge flocks which resemble at a distance swarms of mosquitoes or drifting smoke."

To the Eskimos these little birds are of primary importance. They net them with long-handled nets as they fly over their breeding cliffs and store them in the frozen ground for winter food. Eskimo women gather their eggs, where their nests are found between the rocks and stones, beginning in June. They also use their skins for a birdskin coat called a *tingmiaq*. For one such coat about fifty skins are needed. Admiral Donald B. MacMillan, the Arctic explorer, has de-scribed — in a passage quoted by Forbush — how much the spring arrival of the dovekies has meant to the Eskimos: "But what is that great, pulsating, musical note which seems to fill all space? Now loud and clear, now diminishing to a low hum, the sound proclaims the arrival of the true representative of bird life in the Arctic, the dovekie, or little auk (*Plautus alle*). The long dark winter has at last passed away. The larder open to all is empty. The sun is mounting higher into the heavens day by day. Now and then a seal is seen sunning himself at his hole. The Eskimos are living from hand to mouth. And then that glad cry, relieving all anxiety for the future, bringing joy to every heart, '*Ark-pood-e-ark-suit! Ark-pood-e-ark-suit!*' (Little auks! Little auks!)."

Arctic foxes also depend on the dovekies for food, as well as their immaculately bluish white eggs. Dovekies are preyed upon by ravens and gyrfalcons too, but the big, persistent enemy of which they are in mortal fear is the glaucous or burgomaster gull.

The nitrogen-rich guano of the dovekies, filtering down through the massive hillsides of loose bare stone, fertilizes a deep growth of moss in brilliant green bands. This and other plant life supports hare and ptarmigan and is probably good pasturage for what was once an abundant population of caribou. And in the sea this little bird that makes for provision in depth, both good and cruel, is often eaten by white whales, large fish, and seals.

What a major burden for one so small! Millions of dovekies feed their young during the nesting season and a whole Arctic world depends that they be successful, on and on into the future. The little ones are constantly hungry and chirp in a shrill impatient way until: "the old bird feeds them by disgorging into their bills the content of its well-filled pouch. The consoling, soothing murmur of the old bird to the young, and the satisfied chirping of the young shows how solicitous the one and how grateful the other." Sweet domesticity still keeps the terrible world in order. The little auk is also a tough, all-weather bird, capable of survival in extreme circumstances, and so far it has the room it needs and the isolation and a major range.

How can we predators dare count the bodies, human and other than human, of those on whom we prey! How dare we wipe out whole populations in the first place, either by pulling a trigger or spreading our wastes and poisons by the ton. Still, "dare" may not be the right word for a brutal carelessness so widespread that many men do not dare do anything but trade on it. How many tons of waste go into the air every minute? How much sewage goes into the earth's once pure and flowing waters, or oil's dirty devastation is spread on the seas? How much overkilling will it take for us to come face to face with what is left of the vital innocence that has upheld the world without us up to now, like the dovekie and its Arctic pyramid of needs?

As I watched the dovekies, I saw one come in out of the water, letting itself be washed ashore with the broad sheet of foam sent in ahead of the breakers. It staggered and flopped ahead up the slope of sand beyond the water's reach and stood there. I walked up to the little bird and it made only a slight effort to get away. Its thick breast feathers were coated with oil. They were also stained with the red of its blood. Since oil fouling causes birds to lose the natural insulation of their feathers, and poisons them when they preen, I supposed that this one had been weakened and perhaps flung against a rock by the waves. I picked it up, and what a trembling there was in it, what a whirring heart! I carried it back to my car, thinking to clean the oil off later and see if I could bring it back to health, always a precarious job. But after a few minutes in the heated car the bird's blood began to flow from its breast, to my great dismay, and there seemed to be little I could do about it. I began to feel like a terrible meddler and a coward. With that I took it back to calmer waters, on the bay side of the Cape, and let it go without illusions about the cruel mother that might take care of it better than I, but I felt that my fruitless attempts to save it would be worse. I remember the little beak with its pink lining, open and threatening, as the dovekie protested my picking it up, the black eyes blinking and glistening, the feel of its heart. It was more than a small bird in mortal trouble. It had in it the greatness of its northern range. I had, I suppose, with no excuses for what I failed to do, given it back to its own latitude, to the spirit of choking, roaring waters, of skies with smoky clouds where the little auks themselves looked like smoke in the distance, and of swinging winds and draws between the ice floes, and the rivulets of spring. That bird, which had bloodied me and been so close and warm in my hand, left me on the beach to shake with the weight of human ignorance.

2

IT is still possible, if you have time enough and inclination, simply to watch and wait. All corners of the world that are not so restricted by human pressures as to blind us to them have their revelations still in order. The earth is full of junctions from the past and natural opportunities in the present, whether fulfilled or not. These meeting places may have their mastodons or dovekies, their egrets or their horseshoe crabs, the fossils and their living relatives, the rocks of nearly impenetrable age being washed by the latest waves. In these images, in this unmatched context, nature may take a shape I have never seen before, so I walk out again.

One October afternoon in that season which is a meeting place in itself, a junction of all varieties of migration and change, we took a family trip to Provincetown. The day was sunny and warm and desirable. We climbed over the rolling dune landscape that makes up much of that tip end of the Cape. The clean curved surfaces of the dunes were streaked with beach buggy tracks. We walked up and down and over them to the far shore, across the beautiful landscape swept with great blue shadows and spotted here and there with thickets in hollows, or banked with meadows of beach grass, and the sea visible in the distance. Finally, just before the last fall and rise of dune walls and crests before us, we heard the dry scuttle and snore of the surf.

In the late afternoon there was a bluish, almost opalescent haze on the beach. Sanderlings were flitting, white and gray, along the water's edge, with their look of busy caution. A fishing boat droned offshore and came into sight through the mist that shrouded the sea farther out. Where I was sitting, some twenty feet from the water, a sanderling came along, then slowed down and seemed to half peer at me before hurrying by in front of me. Then a whole flock of sanderlings came swinging in, from low over the water, to land above us, on the middle level of the beach. They were like a white school of fish in their rhythmic, compact unity. And offshore the cloudy waters glinted occasionally with silver from running schools of minnows, otherwise invisible.

We walked back and when we reached Provincetown harbor, there was a red ball of a sun going down over the crests of the houses. Fishing boats were puttering in, one by one, followed by crying crowds of gulls. There was a good deal of activity in the fish-packing establishment at the end of the main wharf. Men were pulling out boxes of haddock from the hold of a boat that lay below the pier, by means of ropes, pulleys and winches. A few dead, gray, striped haddock lay floating in the gas-spotted water around the boat, and a squid, a purplish-pink in color, faded out. The sight of men handling fish, even on a fairly indifferent modern shore, had a certain cold savor to it. The ancient trade of the sea is not hidden yet.

We had supper at a restaurant on the beach overlooking the harbor. A couple of boy and girl waiters, dressed in black and white cotton clothes, summertime help from the city, suddenly deserted the tables and ran out to the waterfront toward a boy with a spear in his hands. I followed them out and there, lying helplessly on its side in the water, was an ocean sunfish, a great black pancake of a fish, a round floating hunk of what looked like tough rubber. Its ventral fin had been sheared off, with the pink flesh showing. There was a spear wound in its side from which blood was seeping out into the water. What cruelty the odd or uncommon brings out in us!

An ocean sunfish, which may grow as large as eight to ten feet long — this one was about four feet — does have to be seen to be believed. It has been called the "head fish," since most of it looks like the extension of its head, with a tail fin amounting to a thick fold of skin at the rear margin of its body. Otherwise, it has two large opposing fins, dorsal and anal, which cannot move back as in other fishes, but have to be waved, or sculled from side to side. The sunfish has a very small mouth on the end of its snout and small eyes. It is said to grunt and groan when hauled out of water.

I could see in that nearly ludicrous remnant of a fish, with the one fin still integral with its back, and the other gone, something that might inspire a boy to spear it, simply because it did not look like anything you should or should not spear. It was ready, like all the injured and castoffs of the earth, for the taking. When the boy pulled the point of his light harpoon out, the fish, with whatever it had left in it of native life and function, veered off dully into the water, while blood poured out and a little flood of water was ejected from its gills. Then I saw, or thought I saw, such rolling despair and final fright in its eyes as to make me want to run away, and there was nowhere to run to, except inside myself and inescapable humanity.

Perhaps the shining fright I saw in the sunfish was more the reflection of a fear in me than anything I could realistically impute to it. That I accept, but there is a living fear which the earth and its animal nature requires, and in its possession men and fish may well belong together. I do not know how to grade the indefinite manifestations between nothingness and consciousness, between that which reacts and that which knows it reacts. I am unable to take refuge in mere guessing, and on the other hand I cannot escape belonging. On that beach I saw a dying fish. I saw its blood and the cool waters beyond it, and the boys and girls laughing, excited, caught up in cruelty and wonder. I saw the random skittering and schooling of the open world's fish and boys, the attraction of men and women to each other, a plunging and joining from birth to death for which none are responsible, out of a simple depth and context unachievable even by those who can create life in a test tube. All were commanded, all helpless, but empowered, with a great world darkness inside them, a fundamental knowing.

XII

Practice In Being

IT may seem that there is no world left but that brand-new one into which we have been thrust with walking wounds, nerves jangling, suffering an outrageous exile from the past. It has even given us a new and more terrible dread than we have ever had before, that the human experiment, self-alienated, self-concentrated, has turned itself into a new kind of unknown, without recourse as well as without precedent. But there is a whole world still as there is a whole life, partly conceived, in any man, and out of it still come nights and days of expectation. There is time to look for correspondence, in the weather or the stars, time to look for connective signs.

I go down to the town landing and look out at the wide landscape of the shore, and I find scope again; it is what comes down from the pole and Hudson Bay, it is what comes meandering up in the warm waters of the Gulf Stream. Take the local elements apart on an easy flowing day, with light winds and little clouds, and expand them, and you know the vast, wind-driven frigidities north of us, graduating southward to tundra, birch and spruce, and you know how the surf crashes on the rocks, and how the vast air masses sweep up from the south carrying the warmth of the tropics with them. The long fringes of the sea run in and out with schools of fish. Birds migrate over the waters. Marine life of all kinds is synchronized to tides and currents, depths and temperatures, the light, the salinity, the time of year. It acts on a given flow of opportunity in terms of each different range of land and sea, each form responding out of a profound history.

All landscape contains the potential world. I have been by possession dispossessed. Possession has thrown place behind, knocked out the ghosts and woodland dreams and their wild enthusiasms and the close war and peace that men have had with local nature. The air is now hazy with impurities; some of the tidewaters lapping in between the grasses take litter or industrial waste with them. The spoiling city is just around the bend. A jet bomber has left a long thin line behind it across the sky like the scar on a stomach. There are lines of jettisoned oil along the beach. The landscape serves as a demonstration of our acts, our adventures with poison, speed and disregard. Still, it is not yet entirely overwhelmed, but takes us with it, insisting on the order and integrity of natural growth. Behind the landscape there remains that scope where the fish run like galaxies in the heavens. And while the seasons change and the weather fronts move through, living things respond with a sureness, delicacy and rhythmic strength. They are the signs, not of any special claim but of a lasting, repeated emphasis on basic capacity, infinite resourcefulness. They say to me that I still have a chance to belong.

Natural events are repeated annually, manifested at much the same time, by a frog's first croaking out of a swamp after the long winter, the winter spawning of a marine fish, the arrival of a swallow, the sprouting of skunk cabbage through February mud. This rhythmic coordination is that of a year, a season, of the earth over thousands of years, of the earth in space. What we call the signs of spring are not merely repetitive, they also testify to an endless allowance and preparedness, in which natural substance and restraint take part. Within this great realm of energy in which there are fires, hurricanes, volcanoes and earthquakes as well, a winter egg or a spring fly are proof of a lasting symmetry and balance which must be the wonder and reliance of the human world.

Some life is always ready for what the breathing, spinning, adjusting earth allows it at any given place. Between the backing and filling of the weather, a hawk flies over, a bud breaks, the dovekies migrate back to the north, ants swarm and jellyfish spawn. Eventually we may even be able to predict all weather with one hundred percent accuracy, as well as change it. But I should hate to know the weather only in terms of prediction, or to have living things so boxed in by human analysis that they would not exist for themselves. Just as we lack sufficient links with it when we merely possess the world, so mere prediction will not encompass the weather. The point is not prediction but practice, the continual exercise of balanced growth toward something which may lie beyond perfectibility.

There is that same rhythmic practice in the weather, producing a spring or winter storm, or the light blue sky with fleeting clouds. When will the storm break, the rain fall, after all that preparation? The clouds gather and recede again, and this may go on all day long, and during the night too, and finally, because conditions overhead are exactly right, the sky covers in completely and after a while the rain falls. There is something of that same kind of gathering and preparation, it seems to me, in the movements of animals, perhaps in everything. Those fish and birds that flock and school have comparable times in which they seem to hesitate, start, return again, gather their forces and finally go on their way. Often these movements seem at random, like the erratic migrations of cedar waxwings. At other times, when a bird pinpoints its nesting site from thousands of miles away and arrives within a few days of when it appeared the year before, some kind of sureness has to be assumed, in the bird itself, and in the way the bird belongs to the order of the earth and its physical nature. In all cases, whether they know what they do and where they are, or whether they go astray and move at random, a faring forth, a circling, a seeking seems to be characteristic of living things. The wheel spins until it finds it place. Even the supposedly passive seed, blown in the wind, only thrives as a plant when it lands in the ground best suited to it. A rock, started in violence, endures the ageless changes of the weather until it may eventually be worn away, but in that it too is part of the active wheeling of the earth. Something chooses, whether it has brains or not, something arrives, out of the grandeur of the whole.

It took me a long time, as I may have intimated earlier in this book, to see the natural world as more than a local phenomenon — the robin on the lawn, the mosquito you swat, the poison ivy you avoid. I have no doubt my failure was due to lack of practice, in me, and in the society that keeps me in tow. Years ago, I first saw freshwater herring, or alewives, migrating up a brook in the springtime, and with some gradual learning on my part I began to realize that they held all earth connections in them, the sun and the moon, the waters of the sea, the land and its downflowing streams. One crowd of silver fish, one stream surface shaking with fins, began to lead me out. For a while I searched from day to day and year to year, and the phenomenon of migrant fish gained more depth as I went on, never far enough. When the fish arrive out of the sea in spring, it is still a first time for me, and I see in them a coming which is more than I understand.

The alewives come in to fresh water to spawn from south to north at progressively later dates, corresponding roughly but unreliably, to a map showing the average last dates of killing frosts along the Atlantic coast. If the first big run of these fish crowd a Cape Cod stream sometime after the middle of April, they may appear in the central part of the Maine coast about the tenth of May. A few come in to Cape Cod in late March, and those left behind, schooling in off-shore waters, apparently move back and forth until the right conditions trigger an impulse in them to migrate from salt water to fresh.

Up in the big tidal river at Damariscotta, Maine, I watched thousands on thousands of them one recent spring as they approached the foot of a stream that ran from a pond down a rocky hillside. The stream waters flowed into brackish tidewater that came and went under a highway bridge, at the entrance to which the alewives were massing before they gradually moved in. A Maine man told me that the north wind had been holding them back from migrating out of the river but that with: "a wind from the southard they come pilin' in."

They were deeply packed and their dark backs hid the bottom of the stream. Just ahead and to the side of the much larger alewives, facing the down-flowing current under the bridge, was a procession of sticklebacks, looking like so many vibrant little leaves pointed at each end. Since the sticklebacks may have been there to eat eggs left on rocks, stones and stream bottom by earlier runs of smelt, one major tribe was coexistent with another, and added to the dimension of the place. The alewives in their deep, shadowy, sinewy advance, their fins angling at the surface, their bodies veering slightly aside where too closely packed, a few circling where they had more room, this grand, blind alliance seemed to move on slowly like a storm. If they had been human beings they might have seemed terribly menacing. There was a readiness in them, an unswerving purpose, a violent sending on which contained the might of the sea. They were messengers of depth. I felt in this mass response, this circling reality, a darker belonging than conscious living knows. It involved no more perhaps than what any man is made of, but it was more, so it seemed to me, than we were currently taking into account.

Intermoving, rushing occasionally, circling, curving and coiling, these heavy fish swam with the kind of flexibility and at the same time contained force characteristic of the moon-pulled tides, of a tornado, ice forming on the shore, the flower moving from its sheath. Also, I saw in their fixed destiny something which I had experienced, as part of a crowd, having to join the army, having to become a part of a war, having to go to school, to be organized, to be disciplined so as to endure, to migrate through calamity. There is a common tyranny in common life, and looking down on the alewives massing in a need to spawn that has no not be turned back, I felt a precariousness that has no end.

2

Six o'clock, here, in the western world, a west unknown to sailor Kolaios, or the porters of Tartessus. Stony Brook ferries its fins to the sea.
　　　　　　　　　　　　—Conrad Aiken, "The Crystal"

THE place I first walked and watched after the alewives was in a small Cape Cod valley, an entirely different environment from Maine. There are very few precipitous descents. A series of ponds have their outlet in a stream called Stony Brook that runs for a short distance down a rocky slope, where fish ladders have helped make the approach gradual, and then the stream meanders gently down the valley toward sand and sea. I keep returning over the years to look for these marine fish along different stretches of the stream, as it runs through salt marsh or cattails higher up, or where the alewives climb the ladders to reach the headwaters, watching their action, their differing motions. When these saltwater fish come in during early spring, especially in the lower parts of the marshland where the inland brook has turned into tidal estuary, and the waters run fairly deep and wide, their bodies seem to lunge as if they still had sea room. They circle and roam with large, precipitous motions.

Further up the valley I have watched groups of them running upstream in shallower areas. They wait in deeper pools, milling about, and then a certain number of them break out to swim in over the sunlit bottom, sometimes scattering wildly, chasing from side to side, then dashing back. Sometimes up to forty or fifty will collect and then go forward together, stopping when they reach another pool shaded by the bank of the stream. Each advance and retreat is like a reconnaissance and then a reinforcement by a supporting group, so that all their simultaneous movements make a brook-long chain of action. Whether I interpret it correctly or not, their momentum seems to me to be self-supplied, in the sense that members reinforce their stimulus to advance. Some will take a long time before continuing up-current on their own, or else they will make separate dashes or forays but keep returning to the group they started out with.

The rhythmic actions of these alewives, remote as they might seem from human experience, has deeply reminded me of human effort. Their skill and its exercise are mute in our terms, and to compare it, say, with the kind of human skills and achievements involved in engineering may be to migrate too far. At the same time some rhythmic analogy may always be valid between any forms of life, if we have a will limber enough to exercise it. I have recognized in their water weaving and advances something from a much younger level in myself. They make me remember when I followed unknowing, when what I experienced was without precedent, when I sensed more than I appraised, when the fresh, wild light of spring drew me ahead, when I was learning without remembering. These perfect, water-and-wind-swept fish, waving like plants with flowery fins, with their clean, light-colored bodies in an identity with water and sandy stream bottoms, still lead me on with brightness and energy. And there is in me a trace of enamoredness with things first seen.

Later on in June, as the spawners are returning to the sea, they often whirl in a confident way, but they are slow in their general movements. They drop back wearily, circling slowly and gradually from the pond outlet to the tide marsh inlet, taking days, perhaps weeks, to finally move out to salt water. The season is rich and full, with the smell of plants, fish and water in the air. There are full-bellied wind sounds down the valley. Leaves hang heavy over the running stream from trees and shrubs along the bank. Pine pollen and algae cover the surface of the water. A few dead alewives turn over and over in the current. At the mouth of the stream the gulls stand on the banks waiting for what small groups of fish may still be coming by. They grunt, make low screams, and almost monosyllabic comments like a resting crowd of people. There is the constant slow wave wash and receding over the sands beyond them, the dark of dampness and the bubbles sinking and disappearing, then the smooth light laving-

over once more. The landscape is running with a
weary power; it has an effortlessness in it like the fish,
but it is heavy with need.

In the full, changing light of the day, I begin to be
conscious that there are still new ways of seeing. A
few gulls fly through a blue hazy air and change my
vision of them a little. Pebbles, bits of sand or algae in
the water, seem to take on a significance I am unable
to interpret. I lie down on my stomach and watch the
fish for a while, where they circle in a pool, a little
closer to them than when I peer down from a bank,
and their insistence is made stronger in me; the mere
sight of those big open eyes, and their still constant if
tired motion, has them endlessly going forward. Also I
begin to see them as a herd, with some of the characteristics of other animals in their unity. When stirred
up the fish crowd skitters and stampedes like buffalo. I
can see the dust.

The water of the stream whirls and eddies down the
valley. Where I look down into it, sticks and leaves
pass by or catch on the bank; they shift, dip and run
with the water. Four little killifish suddenly appear.
They twitch, swim on and flick back, then disappear
downstream. A gull cries overhead and I hear a
northern yellowthroat singing at the edge of the
marsh. These waters are part of a round, a wheel, that
contains the fish holding up against an outward flow,
the waterside-loving warbler, a spider on the surface,
each of them an integral part of the cosmos, each like

a particle of light. Freshwater killifish or marine alewives, alewife fry spawned in the ponds, swim with
the momentum of waters that join sea and land. They
have a sinewy strength that belongs to the swinging
and veering of a million years. I hear the sea sounding, the stream pouring and rustling, behind the sight
of a fish. I see a height of air and water behind the
gull, and an everlasting moving on, with terror and
peace. I see the communal power and trying out of
living things, in conception and act as men define
them, and also in terms of what is given us, an infinite
holding together, unavoidably, proudly, and helplessly
shared.

The landscape moves and changes. The marsh
grasses shine and flow under a skein of clouds. Many
patterns of travel, miraculous modes of light, are contained in this valley. I am invited again to stay. It is
too bad we are always so insistent on leaving real
opportunity behind.

XIII

The Reaches of Spring

SPRING, along this man-occupied shore, begins to force and spread its power like a mushroom upheaving an asphalt road. The light in the cold early weeks of March seems to hover and lift, putting a transcendently new shine on the bare branches and twigs of the trees. I know, in spite of the fact that my human world will not wait, that things are ready, that the alewives wait out in the cold sea, that the trees are ready to transform. The sap will run.

Now comes the second coming, and the thousandth, out of the end of winter, gradual but past catching, the prolongation of an ancient way of change, a holding back and running forward, a gathering and letting go. Here is the spherical earth in a new order with respect to the sun, a new light and a new angle, a constant speed, a continual evolving, out of a million years or a minute. The weather hangs between northern cold and southern warmth. The ice begins to break up. After rain the welcome sunlight glistens over everything and we are lifted up, by one simple, predictable, still viable reaction to spring's release.

Backward glances are inevitable. If only to hold on, if only to see what it was that led up to any one day — still the special day of all days in the year — I am obliged to reconstitute it to some extent out of the past. The light, and my life with it, swings by inexorably. In the northern hemisphere despite the "first day of spring" which may be any one of a number of days and chosen times for millions of people, living in different climatic zones, the process of regeneration has no certain date. For some animals it may begin in the winter sea, with its relatively stable temperatures. The whole wheeling year is a single and at the same time indefinite process, so that the blowing blossoms of the shad, white, delicate and full as clouds, that bloom toward the middle of May in Massachusetts and a week or two later in Maine, have their connections with melting ice at the end of February. But general exactness has its place, seen in detail, heard in pronouncements like the singing of a redwing in a marsh. At the same time, spring, an interval between summer and winter, so that it seems to have passed too quickly between the two, is not allowed in full "pleasance" without the tornados, the freezing winds, the raging of the sea.

When the redwings arrive there is a dusty haze inland from the sea. One black bird with red chevrons on its wings flies low over the dead stalks in a salt marsh and calls it spring. The day before, the sea made a thunderous rim along the sands, with pluming, flowering, plunging breakers ending in steam and smoke along the whitened shore. The storm ended. The sky cleared up after a gentle new wind and turned light blue.

Everything seems to declare its readiness, and then the sky clouds up again. There are blizzards in Omaha, new storms coming in our direction from west, north, and south. The spring peepers finally begin to sing in lowland bogs and wet places, only in a few at first, then in more, almost ready for the full and universal chorus, their "De Profundis Clamavi." Then the temperature drops into the twenties again. The peepers' high, sleigh-bell acclamation is stilled.

If the total amount of heat for the entire earth received during the course of a year from the sun were not in exact balance with the amount lost by radiation and reflection during the same period, the temperature of the seas and of the atmosphere would change drastically and ruinously. What a precise and nearly inconceivable containment that implies, where all acts the year around take part, and how dependent is the human race! At the same time how vulnerable we make ourselves, acting like furies to tip that balance over everywhere.

The spring roots, more surely than mankind, start to probe again; plants blossom at varying times; the peepers sing early while green frogs and bullfrogs croak at a later date; and the birds arrive, progressively later, beginning with the redwings, and continuing with phoebes and tree swallows to the shorebirds and the terns. Under that huge luminary in the sky, the first wildflower blooms — the center, exact in growth and division, of the whole earth's tidal give and take.

As the great light widens in the northern hemisphere, regeneration is in the air. It shows in the ground like luminous green moss in melting snow, or the cooing of mourning doves with their little heads and skinny necks, and evening-blue and beige feathers steeped in iridescence like rainbow foam along the sands. How many ways are there to see things? As many ways as there are men on earth. We could look down into the smallest stream and find ourselves in stream-expression indefinitely. Every watery whirl, each turn and shift in the current, might mean a practice in enlargement. But I admit I have to do a sort of vanishing act just to begin to see. I have to go over to another side, passing through walls of human presumption. Strange that I should have had to do so much just to admit birds and fish into myself. I have had an education in neglect.

The progress of spring breaks through, if anything can, so that our egoistic power of manipulation might be tempered by the real desires of growth. Perhaps the spring will give us the means to re-educate ourselves.

At the very least a resurrection not in our hands opens the range of choice in an excluder's world; and it puts us on a level with all its births and deaths, wherever they occur. The season calls for equality, and says that there is no plot of ground or stretch of water which is not a center of global importance. We may not be faithful to the spring, but we have been given our chance.

I walk out toward the shores of a nearby pond while a nuthatch, head pointed up on the trunk of a pitch pine, with its mate nearby, sings a rapid, nasal: "Up, up, up, up, up." When I climb down steep banks to the little round pond below there is a brazen trumpeting of many blue jays. They sound like a crowd on New Year's Eve, all tooting away at once in the trees around the pond. As they dip and plane through the treetops, stopping in the branches, then flying on, their piping, whistling and horn-blowing honestly sounds as though it were in honor of a celebration for its own sake. Suddenly the interpretation of their calling resolves itself for me into a blue jay's need, not only to communicate with but even to arouse attention in its fellow jays. There is no use my arguing about whether a bird's song is a question of spontaneous reflex, triggered impulse, or not. My sense of the matter is that the organic depths of any intricately aware, individual race, full of unknowns and intangible variants, must disprove mechanics to begin with. And the more unknowns we consider the better for us.

There is a slight shift in the wind, and I get a blessed smell of water from the pond. A few buffleheads fly up when I approach through a grove of pitch pines, circling the pond once, then going into a skidding landing, feet first, farther out in the water. These little saltwater ducks begin to migrate from their wintering grounds along the coast at this time of year, and often stop over in freshwater ponds and lakes for a few days or even several weeks.

I stay where I am for a while, in the green pitch pines, watching and listening. Snow melts from the branches and needles of the trees, dripping down to wet, soggy snow on the ground. The soft outlines of their trunks reflect in the water, with blurred red and pink shrubs, their shapes reversed. The small pond is a silvery lens close-bordered by the reflections of earth, centered on the sky. The buffleheads, eleven of them, chase each other over the surface, making little chattering, squawking noises, or almost chickenlike cluckings. A male rushes toward a female and as she ducks under the water he is right after her. Streaks in the water, an outline near the surface, show their underwater play. The males keep bobbing their puffy heads, with the large white patches on them, making their little rushes after the females or other males. They duck down into the water to come back again like corks, or they may stay down feeding up to about twenty-five seconds, according to my count. Now and then one of them will quit its ducking and short rushes to bathe, vigorously working its tail covers up and down, with much splashing, while it rocks forward and bobs back.

Sometimes the pond is half full of circles and patches from their continual flurries and chasing. They bob and spin, rush by each other and flip under the water. Then the whole flock flies up with great speed, almost springing in flight across the surface, with one last surprising up-banking before they lower down and land. Occasionally, they burst and scatter out ahead for a short distance as though a small fire bomb had been thrown between them. There are intervals when the flock floats calmly on the surface, with slight movements here and there, one half circling another or slowly cruising by. Then the spontaneous play starts again. A black duck I had not noticed flies nearly straight up from the farther shore, with a harsh dry quacking, and the buffleheads stop, look and listen for a few seconds before resuming.

I have become very fond of these perky, charming little birds, as I watched them, and conscious too of how much all their spontaneous acting means in terms of watchfulness, escape, feeding, closeness, spring courtship, the need to migrate and reproduce their kind. Their actions take their measure from many alliances. Each quick turn, every flutter of a feather is associated with the water and earth around them, and the earth beyond them. Whatever function or attribute we may give them as a race of birds will probably never come close enough to their particular sensitivity, which is more than instrumental, having at least the quality of music vibrating in the light, sending waves across the willing air. Things go toward each other. This water home for buffleheads is mine if I go toward it and allow it to receive me, so that I too can act.

The little flock moves out all at once, though I have noticed nothing that could alarm it, whirring straight off the water, then circling the pond three times, gaining altitude as it goes. The buffleheads fly off with a very fast wingbeat, in keeping with the speed and stir with which they manage watery places, earth distances. They go northwestward toward big gray clouds bordered with sun-whitened masses moving across the sun, and disappear. They have left me with the wind in the pines, the pond waters lapping slightly along the shore, a blue jay's piping, and the sense of a new modality. There is much the same kind of cohesive force in their racial union, within which they perform, joining and chasing, as there is in a burst of spray, in schools of fish or groves of trees, and the societies of men are no exception.

2

"Spring is delayed," we say, or "We never have any spring, only winter and summer." But we are wrong. Our failure is in not belonging to it. Otherwise we would see that in spite of all the blows of the weather and a sky closed in, the rhythms are on schedule, modalities increase. Readiness, in all innocence, is free to move, regardless of the frost.

These days carry a perfect stillness between the violence of floods, the breaking up of ice and nations. A tall quiet starts up from the ground, white at dawn, through misty gray mornings, an opening with light. There is a smell of fish and salt marshes and water in the cool air along this length of the world's shore. Spontaneous, unerring conjunctions are beginning to declare themselves. One March afternoon along a Cape Cod beach the gulls, including a good many ringbills, are flying back and forth and round and round, crying, yelping, yowling, dipping into shallow waters and picking up clam worms. Spring has sent the worms out swarming, free-swimming, sinuously moving out through tidal water from the sand, and the gulls have met them. The heavier herring gulls land in the water and scramble after their food. The lighter ringbills pick it up more deftly. Flying low, with bent wings, they dip and take, their heads moving as they look from side to side hunting over the shallows, giving short, repeated cries. High over the silvery-green excited shore, more gulls cry out and circle, or hover in the fresh east wind; and along the line of dunes at the head of the beach a sparrow hawk holds against the wind with great fluttering energy until it allows itself to be swept on. Grass-sweeping, sand-spattering, the wind off the water is a diver and a hoverer in itself.

Through a gray cold haze, up through the suspense of spring, responding to its resolution, the song sparrows chip-chip and trill round and out, bright, bold and clear. On sunny days the chickadees begin to utter their tripartite calls: "fee-a-bee!" or " here pretty!" with more lilting abandon. I hear one tapping away with its sharp black beak at a sunflower seed which it holds between its feet on a pitch-pine branch, and the sound is as loud as a woodpecker tapping on a tree. (Acoustics also change with the spring.) If I were to spend enough time at it, I might begin to grasp the outlines of a distinctive chickadee language. It seems to me that there are many individual versions of the dominant call. Some birds sound it harshly, others softly. They lisp it, they upend it, they sing it on a straight level. They also have a slurred trill with five or six notes involved, and there are whisperings between them, a very light talk interrupted by single "tiks" and split whistles. I have no way to analyze any of their notes and calls, except to try and tie them down to a few recognized behavioral responses; but at the very least they seem to be expressing feeling of a special kind, stimulated by days that now spread outward with a feeling of their own. When a strange-shaped insect moves across this page as I write, with its two antennae flickering in front of a head and thorax that are tiny in proportion to the abdomen that follows behind, an eloquent silence is added.

The fact that most men live lives of noisy desperation, to modernize Thoreau, and even that human society jumps and sizzles on the earth's surface like fat in a frying pan, does not affect the storms, the days of widening light, spring in its inexorable attainment. But in a season of birth there is a risk, which is: not to be born. Indifference will destroy us, not the trials of experience.

Local floodwaters from rivers and streams swollen by spring rain take the debris of the dumps with them, from hundreds of New England cities and towns. In Utah, near an army test site for biological and chemical warfare, the papers report that herds of sheep, some fifty-six hundred of them, have died from some unknown poison, later admitted to be nerve gas, at a cost of $300,000. In the meantime, a great uncounted number of mammals, birds, plants and insect species essential to the earth's ecological balance, continues to be poisoned, driven out, eradicated, or even for a time dangerously overpopulated; and who is attaching the values of the great God Money to *them*!

As part of my random spring research, I read a science news article about dolphins. Because of the exceptionally large brain capacity of this lovely, playful animal, and the resulting publicity, we have been indulging ourselves in all sorts of nonsensical speculation about conversing with them, we in our Donald Duck language, and they in theirs. The U.S. Navy has become interested in the dolphins' exceptional sonar sounding ability, and there is talk of having them tied to missiles so as to detect and blow up enemy submarines. Do we congratulate the dolphins for what human greed will never reach, their body's grace, the incomparable beauty and mystery of their minds?

We rabid exploiters, we predators of the absolute, may think we have no time to dally long with tenderness, as we always have too much at stake. But it is none too soon to fall in line with creation's sparrow, its dolphin, or its osprey.

One day the wind blows cold across beaches and beach grasses on the open fringes of the Atlantic, for hundreds of miles. I walk off a Long Island beach onto a parking lot which has an area of bare ground in the middle covered with low clumps of winter-cropped grass, and out of the corner of my eye I see a horned lark fly down over a bare patch that seemed to move slightly because of something in it. And there my companions and I find three baby larks, hatched about three weeks previously, the date being April 5. The nest is in a slight depression between the grasses, just enough to keep the young birds well hidden below the top level of the ground. The wind blowing over the parking lot lifts up the brown feathers on their heads and backs, and blows the down that sticks out from them in stray white tufts like the fine, silky hair on the head of a very old man. Their little bills open in a futile way as we look at them, showing the pink gape of their mouths. This bare place next to the rough sea, usually defined in terms of summer crowds and traffic, now centers on three baby birds, their making and their sending forth — an elemental three, very small and quiet, cowering under the world winds, a perfection, about to take part.

Birth takes place under pines and spruce that seethe as they are run through broadly by the wind, and under still nights where frozen ground is lighted by the moon, and through storms with flying wet snow, dirty, churning seas, sand along the shore hissing, and the rocks, wind and surf moaning together.

Planktonic creatures twitch, swing back and forth, dart and spin in the cold sea waters. A female stickleback, netted in a salt marsh estuary and put in an aquarium, has a belly that is dark pink with its load of eggs. The fish hovers under a bunch of seaweed in one corner, looking for all the world like a self-concentrated, pregnant female. In the water of ponds and streams countless eggs from fish and frogs and snails begin to appear — eggs in life-giving, life-permitting water, counterparts of the round body of the world. The embryos of frogs make their eggs, embodied in gelatinous strings or masses, alive with motion. Each embryo twitches and spins in its jellied surroundings, each one has two prominent black eyes, as if earth depended first of all on vision, or a later growing up to balance vision.

Water is where life began. From the round cosmos of the egg life is sent forth, into the sea, or out into dry land and through the atmosphere to learn and to adapt, but never without some moisture. Life requires water, adapts itself in extraordinarily refined ways to its absence or insufficiency, and can even wait for it for a long time, like those tiny organisms that can stay dehydrated for months and are then revived by a drop of rain.

Now we are waiting, in the cold air of March and April, not only for some pleasant sunshine, but also for what earth releases from its reservoir of power and substance. No doubt we need an extravagance of eggs in their context of almost numberless provision, like everything else. We need the measured fury of regeneration. We need what is sent forth to consume, and is in itself consumed. We need the flow of water, air and light and the intricate, organically woven stirrings in the soil, because the burden of proof on all life is an unqualified release, which we are in no position to deny.

The frame of emergence is not limited to the grass starting to turn green, or the castings of patient, essential earthworms now appearing on the ground, or the oncoming of migrant fish, but includes major complexities of feeling and response. I see one chickadee suddenly fly toward another, hovering, fanning its wings first slowly, then very fast, and at the same time uttering harsh, repetitive notes. What elements of courtship, of begging or aggression has it revealed? Fly at me, little bird, and tell me more.

One night I almost hit a muskrat with my car. The headlights show it ambling in the rain, with a strange slow gait, half humping and sidling. What has moved it out of the savage stress and restrictions of winter to change place, to wander, to change its feelings, to want more room for need again?

Another night a coon lets out a hair-raising scream outside the house. I go out and follow it as it jumps and scrambles through thickets, down banks between the trees, giving out a wild, agitated, strangled screaming all the while. Spring passions have seized it.

Then one evening late in April a whippoorwill sounds for the first time, in a fluted, whistling, repetitive signal of spring, archaically deep and haunting. Searching for it outdoors, in the dim light, and fooled by the way its call comes from around house, rocks and trees, I set off in the wrong direction, to have the bird suddenly fly up behind me like a huge moth, twisting and hovering, with its tail down, on which the white markings show clearly.

One afternoon I heard a swishing in the grasses down in a partially wet swale behind a line of dunes that faced the sea. A big snake, a black racer, suddenly slipped out, and, head up, flung itself across the bottom of a ditch, with a combined lithe leap and slide, in proud abandon. Such a lordly motion I have never seen equaled. What can approach this primal excellence in snakes?

Spring throws out beauty, speed, ancient needs, death and desire on the land, while we deny it its majority. Perhaps we lack the means to project ourselves. The legendary lands where men once associated human attributes with animal life lie under the sea. Therefore the eagle is no longer a lord of creation, the lion has lost his pride and the ox its patient endurance. Subliminally, man's heroic and sacrificial terms may be struggling for an outlet, but we appear to have discarded our ancient symbols and taken to substitutes made of the base coin of the realm. Still there is something heroically unalterable about the spring. And when I hear those old languages emerge again, in a frog or a bird, when I see wild knowledge in an animal's eye, when I feel, at last, the earth begin to slide and breathe under my feet, I am not sure that we ourselves, even in our will and conscious ability, were not included in the embryonic vision of the year.

Now the trees begin to grow their lightest, smallest leaves, about to expand from delicacy to a summer's endurance, and a softer, warmer wind wells up. An ovenbird flies past me in a wood and seems to give me a startled, backward-glancing look as it goes. Then it lands on a branch close by and immediately sings out in the most abstracted way as if I were not there at all.

Whatever I see, or think I see, advent is foremost and clear enough. Out of overwhelming vitality and order the ovenbird takes its place, the new yellow-green, pink and silvery leaves of the oaks droop tenderly, the catkins hang, and the handsome stiff plumes of the cinnamon fern arise. The parasite moves to its host; the tick waits on the grass. The migratory birds come in and prepare to mate, or move on, others begin to nest and feed and behave with that sure but complex interaction with their environment which all students of life must marvel to see.

The trees that now become youthful again with leaves invite old, evolving patterns of use, of coming together, and also of the senses. The wood I wait in moves from a roadside edge with open sunlight, across a hollow and up its surrounding banks. There are briers, poplar and red maple on lower levels, then pitch pine and oak climbing the slopes, giving the wood different assemblies of light and shade that must be of great significance to the life that uses it. A yellow-shafted flicker stops by a hole in a tree, hesitantly, then flies off. Towhees, with their tails spread, fly in low over the ground. A white and gray gull, out of all wood particulars, soars in the blue between the treetops. Another little greenish-backed ovenbird comes walking and bobbing over the wood floor, a welcome sight for other reasons than its association with spring. Because of pesticides dripping off the leaves and poisoning their food, only a small number of these wood warblers still nest in this area compared to what there used to be. I have marked their disappearance, and I know.

For at least an hour, I watch a downy woodpecker working at a hole in a dead pine, bringing out sawdust in its bill, shaping the hole's edge from time to time with the concentration of a true artist. Then a female arrives, and they copulate, with the female on the end of a limb and the male bent backwards in contact with her. Then she flies off and he works on the hole for another half- to three-quarters of an hour until his mate returns and they both fly off together.

Suspense is still with us, obduracy and hesitation, then fury rises in the wind, leaving limp flowers, blowing off the leaves, and rocking the trees so that their roots can be seen rising and straining under the surface of the ground. The sea roars, wet snow falls, but spring endures. A hermit thrush peals out of the oak woods one evening, up through glistening, silvery trees and its song means the advent of another distance to me. It is an old-new swirl of sound, the answering of bells, to be answered or not, a returning. I go on waiting. Then I hear the inevitable bright, spiraling notes, part of a lifting light, part of the swirling and tinkling of water in a northern stream, the reach of a tree, a matter of fact exultation in the shadows.

The expansion of spring is an expansion of delicacy, touch and complexity like the growth of a tadpole from its egg. Vision and visibility increase in a region tight and battened down for half the year, and so do all the casualties of a new existence. Alewives die, torn on rocks or killed by gulls in their inland migration. Nests are blown off trees by the winds and the young birds die on the ground. Out in the blue and green waters along the shore, the tempo of wings and fins, the excitement of hunger and desire, rise immeasurably. One day a huge fin-backed whale, some sixty feet long, comes close to the shore at high tide, then moves off and returns at high water, and is finally beached. The sick, now dying, whale lies in bloody pools at the sand's edge, its superb tail moving slowly up and down, a dull brownish eye moving, blowing occasionally with a ponderous sad sound. Inland, a mother woodchuck is shot and its cold, deserted young ones die. There are trembling, shaky, baby rabbits in the leaves and in the grass, vulnerable to all kinds of predators.

The wide, warm-blowing new world is tender to the young, it is made out of darkness unlimited; it lunges precipitously like ravenous fish; it slips swiftly through the sky like a tern. At night whippoorwills by the dozen sound in the woods, with layer on layer of shouting song. Cold, wet hours follow, then nights with soundless soundings among the stars. Evenings are full of spirit fire like the feathers of a Blackburnian warbler, and ceremonious action, like the gulls that wait at dusk along the shore, strutting around each other, and flocking in circles overhead. Grand assemblies and fatalities, mood after mood, risk after risk, come into place. Like a thunderstorm in preparation, subsiding and coming on again, the season employs its prodigality, up to that controlled limit in the heat of early summer when the pollen stops blowing, the spring wind dies down, calm seas follow, growing life hunts and endures.

We share in this tremendous commitment, even in our own lavish use of it. While the blood of the sea runs as fresh as the juices in the plants and the pulse of living things beats high, the soul of the human world endures new trials. Every instant our being burns with infinite complexities. The context of the humanized earth is seething with change and disaster and renovation, for have we not been led by reckless springs for thousands of years to live in a wild way? It is a wonder the globe can hold us; in fact we may have gone too far already for it not to shrug us off. But by the same token we have the deepest need for all earth's measured balance, everything its calmest powers can provide.

The volcanoes of energy will boil again. But as the landscape of natural increase is being thinned out and impoverished by human use, so we too can be impoverished, and not in that honest poverty which is shared by the bluebird and the meadow mouse, the man who lives life on its own ground, the life that meets daily with all creation in equality. Creation after creation is in us. The Apollo spacecraft and the jet plane, the structure of atoms, the symphony and the poem, the ability to build and to destroy, have us whirling off like the spheres, but without obligation we are nothing. Cosmic discipline will not allow too much ignorance of what it cherishes.

Spring is an unparalleled happening, a manifestation of ancient levels and meanings freshly tried out, another throw at things, though its universal measures never let those wild fires get completely out of control. The light of spring comes to us in our puzzlement and self-concentrated agonies as if it could only be seen by the exemplary eye in every man, the witness to what is incomparable, an everlasting, sacred commitment running through all things.

XIV

The Eye of the Heart

And when he came upon a great quantity of flowers he
would preach to them and invite them to praise the
Lord, just as if they had been gifted with reason. So also
cornfields and vineyards, stones, woods, and all the beauties
of the field, fountains of waters, all the verdure of gardens,
earth and fire, air and wind would he with sincerest purity
exhort to the love and willing service of God. In short he
called all creatures by the name of brother, and in a
surpassing manner, of which other men had no experience,
he discerned the hidden things of creation with the eye of
the heart, as one who had already escaped into the glorious
liberty of the children of God.

—Brother Thomas of Celano, *The Lives of
St. Francis of Assisi*

I GO down to the town landing again on the shore
that has opened itself to me over the years and been
an introduction to the earth. I hear the thunder of
water, the thunder of a plane in the sky. The sun's
radiance, though less direct now that summer goes,
still warms the shallow seas. There is a brave honking
of Canada geese over the land. Migratory birds skim
along the shoaling sands. Here where there is an open
balance of many worlds, I can also sense the massive

interventions of mankind, our terrible amputations and distortions. But the tides change with their wonderful rhythmic grace, and life moves with them. As the tide began to ebb during the afternoon, with a simultaneous beating in and pulling back of low waves, a hundred gulls flew out from the salt marsh creek back of the beach, crying, moving back to waters now getting shallower, where they could more readily find food. It was a correspondingly rhythmic, well-timed, steady move. And so these backings and fillings, the going and returning, ripples in sand, a roaring sunset, a gray and showery dawn welcomed everywhere. Spring followed an ice age, the tropics arrived, a new ice age will be accepted in its time. The earth-tried enormous balance puts the whir of a fin and the shock of a hurricane together, and accepts all sinewy, kinetic, visionary response, and the inner darkness of sense as men know it — and the deliverance from sense.

Nature is something I have never wholly seen before. That is more than an assumption, because I doubt that there has been a day in all my natural life that mere repetition was all that was provided me, in spite of monotony, in spite of my own readiness to sleep rather than act, or actively receive. In the second place, whatever happens to me by night or day, at whatever age, comes not altogether of my own volition. The real nature of causation is largely unknown to us. What part are we really playing in the creative universe? Behind the beauty, the savagery, the minnow, or the leaf, there is that which plays with *us* like light on a wing and is just as uncatchable.

None of us seem to get the chance to see enough in order to rightfully enlarge our lives before their end. But we have a history in us which is of the earth, and nature gives us clues to its capacity, and signs now and then of the incomparable form and passion in which we take part. I remember, when I was in Nova Scotia, heading for Newfoundland, that I passed by a woods fire on the way to the airport. It was only a small fire and the local fire department had almost managed to put it out. The men were concentrating their hose on the ground at the base of a tall spruce, the last to go. The fire shot up in a deeply roaring, devouring orange-red wave. Then it topped the tree with a final rush and fury. A one last crackling curl into the air and it was gone completely, leaving a tall, smoking black stick with naked branches behind. In a country of frequent forest fires, this was not a memorable event, but for me it provided an added, elemental statement, flung out against the background of an ancient world.

Exaggeration, so many artists say, is a necessity in expression. The wild, the mad, the hyperbolean puts the passionate point across. But we are deceived if we think that our exaggeration goes any further than in nature. Follow that fire, that wild heave of wind, the enormous cloud range on the horizon, the evenings of burning cold, mornings a cave of darkness, days with hissing snow, all expressing the inexpressible, and how far do you get? The brush has barely touched the canvas.

I do not live in a backwater, not in *this* world. This is a shore, not of a pond or marine embayment, but of the globe. Man has made it that way. You have to give us some backhanded credit for universality if only in the sense that we occupy the entire globe, and cannot leave each other alone. And not too far from me is the city I came from, which is a mystery in itself, though an often tortured, smoking, gasping one. How did the unbelievable quantity of material that makes up those vast towers ever get into the city in the first place, under the cover of darkness?

I came out of the dark mouth of the subway in late evening and watched the sky turn sulphurous above a city square. It was like an artificial sea. White and scarlet signs, fat with glass, hung overhead, and I walked past yellow caves with music jangling at their entrances, through waters of light. During the day rivets tapped up and down on steel spines, trucks fumed and ground their gears, brakes squealed, there were sounds of upheaval and crashing as walls were building up and tumbling down, and in between, those stops and silences in which heels are heard clicking on the sidewalks. The city is a storm, a place of floods, a flood of lights, of intense, competitive friends, intense loneliness. The city is a tide, though without much mathematical predictability, and what spreads out from the city and touches all the natural world is not so much a remoteness, an artificiality, as a power, even a massive kind of blindness which takes its impetus from relentless social conflict. In the city, "Know thyself" becomes "Know thy world," or take the consequences; and, theoretically, what happens to the osprey or the peregrine is out of the picture. But if you believe that true bonds in nature are not external, then our meetings with it are on the central square, or 37th Street (where I grew up), as well as on this beach being cleaned by autumn winds; it is only that our human commitment and its terminology are in dire need of extension. Perhaps we lack the images whereby to save the natural world through our own organic and moral connection with it — at the very least the old pastoral images will have to be reconstituted. This may be in the hands of science, of psychology and biology, but in order to bridge the gap between science and the general understanding, natural phenomena need to be treated as of a life to a life. Our overriding concept ought to be that in the wholeness of the living environment there can be no exclusions.

Extra-human, extra-natural terms divide us from compassion. We have a death-dealing capacity that is without parallel; and, having to a large extent disorganized the gradual, assimilated experience which bound man to place, we have thrown events not only into the hands of unpredictable change but into the unknown capacity of mankind to keep control without appalling tyranny. We are governed by our obsession with means. We have been treating the earth with a recklessness which is no tribute to human genius. The almost total poisoning of the natural environment is only being postponed by fragmentary efforts.

The great danger in a revolutionary world that takes us with it in spreading mobility, forced communication and unprecedented speed, uncertain of the outcome, is that we will take our own risks and live out our own violence as we can. In other words, we may risk the habitable earth for the sake of mere impetus. Perhaps the awareness of disaster will prevent us from bringing on our own artificial ice age which could postpone spring for ten thousand years. Perhaps we can, by conscious, continual effort, keep turning the bow aside to save the ship. We will have to try, in this one world. We have now come to the point where we meet the living earth either in terms of fundamental conflict or fundamental cooperation. All our pillaging and presumption have brought us face to face with ultimate limits. We have pushed ourselves and the rest of life on earth to a point where one step more could mean survival or extinction.

On the other hand, the revolution we are now making only increases the frustration, the greed and longing in our lives. I am still passion's slave. I still cannot fully discover why I act the way I do. I am still frightened by my human reach and its ties with human misery. I know by an experience I never conceived that I do not, and never have, lived to myself alone. And there, next to me, as the east wind blows in early fall, a season open to great migrations, are those lives, threading the air and the waters of the sea, that come out of an incomparable darkness, which is also my own. To claim a false connection from a distance would be to fall prey to a far worse fate than being born and growing old. Universal inclusion is the best and worst we will ever know. In John Donne's words, spoken in St. Paul's Cathedral: "As the Lord liveth, I would not have thee dye, but live, but dye an everlasting life, and live an everlasting death. . . ."

Off over the shoals in the bright afternoon, now that the tide has nearly ebbed and shallow waters run with schools of small fish, the gulls are flocking and dipping in, crying out in wild, shivery tones. The wind makes the green and gold marsh grasses hiss, nod and sway. The clouds over the sea look like fine filamented seaweed swaying lightly in the water. A flock of terns, lined up into the wind on the banks of the outgoing creek, suddenly fly up excitedly at nothing more than a sudden small wave, a rush of water in the current running by them. Then they fly down again, facing up the sandy slope, each in an orderly spacing with respect to the other. Those which were first to land are nearest the water and the rest take their positions above them.

The water flows by, with waves in the sky and in the season, part of the wheels of the year, and when the tide turns again it is scarcely noticeable. Whatever instability may occur in natural circumstances, or is introduced by human agency, motion itself is the great stability.

In the late afternoon, several hours after the tide has turned, and the waters that run along the sloping beach are glinting with copper and gold, I hear the sound of fish. Saltwater minnows by the thousand, flipping at the surface, running through the grasses just off the beach, make clicking sounds like grasshoppers in a meadow.

Do men say that fish run without them, and that the tides ebb and flood with an indifference? Are we, in our overwhelming responsibility as the bearers of consciousness, seekers of meaning, without a nod or shake of the head from the universe? But nothing we can ever do is diametric to the sun. We may drive ourselves through power and confusion beyond the outer limits of universal tolerance but the tides continue.

Perhaps this smacks of cold physics, but to share (and that is what the natural environment needs of mankind — at the very least an effort toward mutual accommodation) may mean that we have to find new ways to tolerate the inescapable. After all, these global waters are where we came from. Out of these primal bounds and allowances the mystery of knowing emerged. Out of this life-sea came a being that could express the incredible idea of God in his hawk-headed heaven. Our limits and our possibilities have not escaped their universal origin, their ties in love. Life allows only so much, a certain number of seasons for any man. We are limited, but in major terms. Cosmic participation calls for scope. Reality circumscribes us, and at the same time not only awareness but the experience of living takes each of us on a great journey into space and into a profound, painful acquaintance with the relentless standards of growth and survival; and these are mere words compared with their potentiality. In us there is an infinite play in depth, of reckless encounters, brave effort, hopeless ineptitude, weakness that leads to murder and self-murder. But this is in the order of space, where we live on one earth and its many seas, room from which we will not soon escape.

It is strange, I think, to have survived myself. It is strange also to have come safely through terror and constriction, the tyranny of human means, the fear we have of our own attributes; but something more than getting through has brought me to this shore. Life is endured, and it also steers me. I am kept in a certain organic and spiritual frame, held in cosmic dignity even in my failure at dignity, and this is human, and natural too, as nature is the context for an inexorable discipline, in which I and the frog have our special character and our mortal ends.

Through the inescapable meetings with what we are, or what we may not be, there is all human experience for any man to know, and a way, I think, to meet the rest of life on earth. There is no discrepancy between what makes me go through the same inescapable problems as my fathers, and the vast energies that are put into the readiness of the seed, or the sending of a mouse or bird through a short hard life for the sake of its race. These necessities come out of those down-under continents where indivisible existence was generated. If nature is inside me, with its grace and inevitable demands, I can hardly deny it without excluding myself from most of earth's intentions.

This season in its flowing power is a measure of the whole earth. This putting forth of the gentle and implacable together in the realms of nature, the violet and the shark, of innocence to the ends of maturity, of rising up to send abroad, is part of world weather. And all the sacrifices made along the way are an immolation at one with all identity. Nature is life's creation, life's spending. No amount of intellectual despair, nihilism or sense of worthlessness in men can alter their basic dependence on regeneration, that which sends every beauty, each excellence, in each detail, into everlasting fire. We will not survive without the seeds of grass, and the mass of minute animals twitching in the waters of the sea. We belong to these multitudes; all that is lacking is our commitment and our praise.

It may be that nothing is predictable but the precarious nature of human history; and this may be what the universe provides for us. From these endless conflicts, that tear us apart and throw us together, future standards of cooperation may be born, even out of a need that seems pitiless. We change after all, out of deeper, universal changes, unseen fruitions, the coalescing of elements out of disparate parts; our acts materialize out of an ageless adventuring. But our place in this universal equilibrium needs realistic allegiance, and the exercise of sight, in all humility. In the face of perverse human will, armed with superhuman powers of destruction, we have little time to wait.

How can we be optimistic about a technology that merely speeds us beyond our inherited capacity, in terms of genetics and physical attributes, to survive on earth? We cannot change the environment past the degree to which we are able to change ourselves. We cannot adapt to continual alterations of our own making that destroy our sources in natural energy and diversity. It is already obvious that technological changes are at variance with our ability to keep up with them, that we are falling into violence, mistrust and confusion. We are in no position to boast about a manipulated future. The pride we need is something else.

A viable future needs its champions, those who will defend not only their own self-interest but function and belonging in nature. The future can be an entirety or a fragment. Divisions can breed divisions, as enemies breed enemies, until at last the universe will restore unity in what might be a catastrophic way.

Man against the natural world is man against himself. In spite of our rational endowments, we are now acting toward our earth environment with the random ferocity of bluefish attacking a school of herring. The equivalent greed in nature at least acts on behalf of fecundity. What is eaten up is a measure of reproduction, but we, with our limited and short-term means, are unable, all by ourselves, to make up what we consume.

Somewhere along the line, the demand exceeds the supply. Starvation and violence occur. This happens in human society. It is happening with respect to man's relationship with nature, now; and so long as we treat nature as a commodity instead of a life-and-death companion, the worse things will be.

As an old countryman in Vermont once said to me: "Ain't any of us know too much." That seems to be the soundest philosophical position a man could take, but, as he was talking about himself and a college professor at the time, I think he was really saying that each man has his validity. Each man has his democratic validity on behalf of his world, and how much he can speak, live and act in terms of its potentiality, but that world in isolation from nature is a world devalued. We cannot live in the full use of earth and earth's complex, expectant, vast experience and deny it at the same time. Worth is defined by participation.

The problem of man's undertaking his own evolution, the risks involved in human achievement and assumption, are not the whole point. The whole point is that we depend ultimately on an everlasting drive for unity whose wellsprings we did not create but can only draw upon or try to re-create. The whole point is the human commitment of human experience to universal nature and all its lives. We cannot divide one from the other, or neither will be sustained. When I look out on the rippling landscape and breathe the lasting air, walking in the right of earth and sun, I am a central part of the globe, humanly claimed, and I also depend on a reservoir of knowing and being forever incomplete. Buried deeper than our microscopes can see, there is a well of flux and motion, incomparable elaboration, a consuming joined with a proliferation, out of which all things are born, are required to be born.

So I go down to the shore again, not only as the old clammers did, day after day, with their own company, but in sight of our crowded world. There is no escaping from our fierce ventures, win, lose or draw, no escaping from resurrections, not only of the seed but human trouble, risk and brutality. These sands not only bear lone walkers and the tide, but all mankind. At the same time, we are also what we choose, by cultivation and association. The natural horizon has in it something that is rarer than sight. It is the source not only of taking and fear but of an unlimited potential beyond the survival of man or fish. We have to keep up with that potential not only in terms of our assumptions about it but in terms of how much we can cooperate, discriminate and cherish.

The earth insists on its intentions, however men may interpret them. Unity and use is what it asks. And use is what may be missing. To the degree that we become disassociated by our power to exploit from what it is we exploit, so our senses will become atrophied, our skills diminished, our earth-related vision hopelessly dimmed. Without a new equation in which natural and human need are together in eternal process and identity, we may be lost to one another, and starved of our inheritance.

sightline books..........
The Iowa Series in Literary Nonfiction

The Men in My Country
MARILYN ABILDSKOV

Shadow Girl: A Memoir of Attachment
DEB ABRAMSON

Embalming Mom: Essays in Life
JANET BURROWAY

*Dream Not of Other Worlds: Teaching in
a Segregated Elementary School, 1970*
HUSTON DIEHL

*Fauna and Flora, Earth and Sky:
Brushes with Nature's Wisdom*
TRUDY DITTMAR

In Defense of Nature
JOHN HAY

Letters to Kate: Life after Life
CARL H. KLAUS

Essays of Elia
CHARLES LAMB

The Body of Brooklyn
DAVID LAZAR

No Such Country: Essays toward Home
ELMAR LUETH

Grammar Lessons: Translating a Life in Spain
MICHELE MORANO

Currency of the Heart:
A Year of Investing, Death, Work, and Coins
DONALD R. NICHOLS

Oppenheimer Is Watching Me: A Memoir
JEFF PORTER

Memoirs of a Revolutionary
VICTOR SERGE

The Harvard Black Rock Forest
GEORGE W. S. TROW